Grace HARBOR

By

DAWN JOHNS

Proisle Publishing Services LLC
1177 6th Ave 5th Floor
New York, NY 10036, USA
Phone: (+1 347-922-3779)
info@proislepublishing.com

ISBN: 979-8-9858816-6-0

And a Man shall be as a hiding place from the wind,
and a covert from the tempest...Isaiah 32:2

Contents

Introduction

My Lord and Savior, Jesus Christ, has been a safe harbor of grace through the storms. I cannot imagine life without Him. I have grown to love Him with all my heart. I was drawn to Him because He first loved me. He pours His love into me so that I might give it back to Him

All along the way, our journey is covered by grace. If we look, we will find it. God loves for His children to talk to Him, to reach out and trust Him and bring Him into our everyday lives. When we do, His grace is revealed to us, and that grace will supply whatever we need, at the time that we need it. Grace is Jesus.

Chapter 1

Finding Grace

I first heard the voice of God when I was about nineteen years old. During my prayer time, the Holy Spirit spoke to my spirit, quietly, "*Stop dating ____.*" A name was mentioned, someone I'd been spending time with. We were not in love, but I enjoyed being with him and I was not dating anyone else at the time. He was a nice guy and went to church. In my own youthful arrogance, I answered God, "Send me someone else and I will stop dating him." God spoke again, "*Trust me. Stop dating _____ and I will send you someone.*" I responded, "Send me someone first, then I will stop dating him." Silence. I had won...so I thought.

Overall, we'd dated for about a year and a half and began to feel very close, but eventually we broke up. The lost relationship hurt, and I wished I had listened to God before allowing myself to care about someone God had not chosen. What I did not realize was that God's grace had kept me from marrying someone who was not chosen for me by Him.

God was speaking to me about not dating at that time as would a father who was protecting his daughter. The Lord knows the end from the beginning, what is going to be the end of a thing even as it is getting started. It would take years before I had some understanding of how much love and mercy was behind all that grace.

God wants us to hear His voice. He expects us to hear His voice:

> "My sheep hear my voice, and I know them,
> and they follow me." John 10:27

Being a follower of Jesus Christ awards us the privilege of one-on-one communion with the Holy Trinity: God the Father, God the Son, and God the Holy Spirit—They are one. We become one with God in the spirit. When we hear His voice, it is the supernatural intercourse with Heaven, something that God means for us to engage in regularly, throughout this life.

Elijah said God's voice was still and small. Ezekiel and John described it as the sound of many waters. Mostly, we hear His voice in our inner man, a voice that we know is not our own. One teenager described it as, "You know it's God when a thought pops into your mind that you know you didn't think of yourself."

Urgings and promptings in us are also ways that God reveals His will to us. God used this way to speak to me at a young age. When I was twelve years old, I attended Vacation Bible School. The teacher told us that she would have the pastor talk to those students who had not accepted Christ as their Savior. Not wanting to draw attention to myself, I felt like I needed to do the right thing, which, according to my teacher, was to accept Jesus. Besides that, I had no idea what the pastor was going to do to those who had not yet been saved!

The next Sunday, I walked up the church aisle and told the pastor I wanted to accept Jesus as my Savior. I had never been under conviction or drawn by the Holy Spirit, but I made my profession public and was baptized. Everyone was so happy—except me. Within days, I realized I had not known about repentance and making Jesus the Lord of my life.

As the Holy Spirit truly convicted me, I knelt by my bed and gave my heart to the Lord. There was one problem: He made it clear to me, in my spirit, that He wanted me to be rebaptized. No way! I had just done that and...what would people think? I would not be rebaptized. For many years of my life, I would continue to struggle with the fear of man and what other people think.

I doubted my salvation, even when I heard God's voice... but I had a strong drawing to Him. I was raised in a Christian family and my mother kept my thoughts directed toward God. Though they did not attend every church service, I knew she was praying for me. I wanted to be in church, even on the days when my family was not. I loved walking to church with the other kids in the neighborhood.

I was especially fond of a large Bible storybook that belonged to my mother. I would pull it down from the bookshelf and carry it to my room, where I could be alone. It was like opening a secret treasure. These stories were true and took up residency inside me, unlike the fictional books I'd read. This hunger and desire for more understanding of God grew throughout adolescence, but I was still disobedient to the urging of the Holy Spirit to be rebaptized.

I would not be obedient to that call until fifteen years later. That act of being submissive to God's will, which I had delayed for so long, would bring a great peace and increased love in me for all people. It would also remove all doubt of my salvation.

The Bible tells us that the fear of man brings a snare—a trap—something from which we cannot free ourselves. When our decision-making is based on what people think over what God is telling us, we are caught and caged, losing our freedom to be all God has made us. Fear of man is wrapped up in pride. We do not want to lose the comfort of being accepted by people. However, pride leads to a fall. Humbling ourselves to God's will brings grace. Our human pride pushes God away. We believe we do not need Him, or perhaps think that our way is better. When we take the first step to walk in line with what we know God has given us to do, grace comes running. Grace will make a way. Embracing the humility to follow God will defeat pride.

Even at a young age, my not obeying God, who was urging me to be rebaptized, was self-preservation on my part. Those acts of disobedience affected my relationship with God. In a way, my carnal nature was offended by God's instructions to me, which were against what I wanted.

The book of Psalms shows us a better way:

> "Great peace have they which love thy law: and
> nothing shall offend them." Psalms 119:165

"Law" stands for God's word, His instruction to us. When we are hungry for the word of God and seeking to receive His guidance, we will not be offended by what He has for us. His word, penetrating our soul, is love, and love does not consider any wrong done to it. Humility takes over and pride is pushed out. No matter how ridiculous the undertaking God has for us might seem to be, acknowledging that we need God and submitting to His instructions for us brings grace. With obedience, pride is defeated, humility steps in, and we are exalted in Heaven's eyes. That is where we find grace.

Chapter 2

Grace for Family

At twenty years old, I met Donald. We dated for a month before he asked me to marry him. Knowing Donald was a Christian and from a Christian family, I accepted his proposal but also realized that, this time, I wanted God's approval.

As we shopped for wedding rings, I asked God for a sign to show me that Donald was the one He intended for me. None of the display rings would fit Donald's unusually sized ring finger. After looking at several sets, I asked God to give me a sign that if Donald were the right one the next wedding band that he tried on would fit his finger. I knew that asking for a sign was not always the best way to find God's will, but I just wanted one more indication that my marriage to Donald was the best path and part of God's plan for both of our lives. Donald knew nothing of my prayer.

There was one set I'd wanted from the moment I saw it, but at the time, Donald had not been interested. He finally agreed to give it a try. As he slid the band onto his finger, it fit him perfectly. I was a little amazed that God had heard and answered my prayer. The sales clerk was even surprised that it fit. I told Donald again that I liked this set the best, he agreed. I will never forget that day when God's grace poured out Heaven's approval of our union.

God has a plan for our lives, and that includes each one of us. I believe part of His plan includes a good mate with whom to share the future. When we ask God for His direction and will, and follow His guidance, the destiny and the very purpose for which we were created will be fulfilled. It does not mean life will necessarily be easier, because we live in a broken world and we are broken people. As we walk with God, we are in the process of being healed, we will be on track with God's plan, and that always ends with peace. The Holy Spirit's peace and grace remain with us, to strengthen us along the way. Reaching out for God's plan and complying with it is also reaching out for His grace, because He gives grace for us to do His will.

When I became pregnant in our first year of marriage, I was afraid I did not have enough love or wisdom to be a parent. I diligently sought God for both. I read everything I could get my hands on about pregnancy and having children. What the Bible had to say was especially important. My prayers were consistent for more wisdom and more love. What kept coming to my mind was that I was going to be responsible for raising a human being and preparing him for life. Not only that, but this new person was going to affect other people too. This was one of life's most important assignments, and love would be the most necessary requirement to carry it out.

I listened to my mother and other friends and family, but mostly God. With each passing month, more and more peace manifested itself in me. When it was time for our little one to come, I felt ready too.

As always, God was faithful. When the nurse laid my son, Andrew Keith Johns, in my arms for the first time, a love like I had never known before engulfed me. I felt tenderly loving and fiercely protective at the same time. He was beautiful in every way! Snuggled close to me in my arms, he fulfilled a missing part of life. It seemed everything was new, even me. Becoming a mother awakened a fulfillment and purpose in me, driven by a powerful love that gripped every cell of my being. I felt peaceful delight. This was the reason for my life, to raise a child with love and for him to know God. Holding my son had washed away all my fear. I knew I would have another child someday. God had answered my prayer for love, exceeding what I could have thought to ask. I loved this child with everything in me.

On March 21, 1983, our second son was born, Matthew Ryan Johns. His birth brought a flood of joy. Even though he cried with colic a good part of his first eleven months, I loved him, and I loved being with him. It was a good thing too, because mostly we both slept in the rocking chair— when he did sleep. I ate with him in my lap, cooked with him on my hip, and sat with him in the playpen. To say we were close would not be exaggerating.

My brave husband came to me one night and stated boldly that he would take care of Matt so I could get some sleep. I do not know if it was the dark circles under my eyes or the short, incomplete sentences in which I now carried out conversations that gave him the courage for such a gallant act, but I was so grateful, although a little skeptical that this would work.

About three a.m., Donald stood beside my bed speaking loudly: "Honey, I can't do this. You are going to have to take him." I quickly shook myself out of the grogginess of heavy sleep, threw back the covers, and stood up, taking a crying baby from his arms. I was not upset that I had to get up so early; I was thankful that I had been able to lay down in the bed and sleep...even for a few hours. I knew God had given me grace with Matt. Not everyone would have that; I was thankful it was me. Holding my babies at night, when it was just the two of us, was a special blessing, even with colic. Nighttime was when strong, loving bonds were formed. Nothing on earth compared to that.

When Matt was eighteen months old and throwing one of his strong-willed fits, I went to my bedroom, dropped to my knees, and, in desperation, cried out to God. "Lord! I don't know how to handle Matt. Andy is so obedient and quiet and easy to raise. Matt is so strong-willed and defiant. Show me what to do!" He immediately spoke to my spirit: "*I can use both personalities. Praise Matt more.*" I was filled with such peace. If God could use both personalities, then I was good with Matt's strong will. But *praise* him more? That took me by surprise. I wanted to discipline him more. I could not see how praise would work, but God knew best, so praise was what Matt would get.

Andy was easy to encourage, but day by day I looked for ways to praise Matt. If he picked up a string off the carpet, I would praise him for cleaning. If he closed a cabinet door, even if he had opened it, I would thank him for helping Mommy. Soon, I was aware of a peace between me and this child who had been seeking my encouragement. We were enjoying each other. Matt was more obedient. The praise had worked. God knew what each personality needed, and

He knew Matt needed praise. I acknowledged God, sought His will, and He was faithful to answer.

Raising these two boys was the joy of my life. I was aware of the great responsibility that had been given me as their mother, and I took it to heart. God gives wisdom liberally when we ask for it, and I was asking for it almost daily. The wisdom and love God gave me in answer to my persistent prayers were evident. There were times people would stop and talk to me in a grocery store or other public place. They would say things like, "You are such a good mother," or "You spend so much time with your children. You stop and explain things to them." It was confirmation that I was doing something right. Of course, family and friends would say things like that, but for strangers to stop shopping or whatever they were doing to come and say something to me was extra special. God knew that I would need those words of encouragement for what I would have to endure.

> "For You fashioned my inmost being, You knit
> me together in my mother's womb. I thank
> You because I am awesomely made, wonder-
> fully; Your works are wonders—I know this
> very well. My bones were not hidden from You
> when I was being made in secret, intricately
> woven in the depths of the earth. Your eyes
> could see me as an embryo, but in Your book
> all my days were already written; my days
> had been shaped before any of them existed."
> Psalms 139:13–16 (The Message Bible)

Each little personality, every gift and future destiny, is carefully chosen for that tiny person before they are ever born. God knows each one individually and He knows them well. They are His and they are formed by Him. He watches them growing in the womb and has planned their eternity before their first day begins. How awesome the Lord is! Because God knows us so well, He knows what we need at the time that we need it. I wanted to know what Matt needed. I asked, and God gave. Every person has a way of relating to others. Each person also has a way that others can best relate to them. God knows what someone needs to hear and what will trigger their ability to respond effectively. There is grace for raising children, and God gives it when we ask.

If Matt cried, Andy cried, but after a few months and the crying continued, it was comical to see Andy lose his empathy and put his hands over his ears to shut out the noise. As Matt grew into a toddler, the colic was gone, but he had developed a great deal of volume through exercising his lungs early. He had become accustomed to loud crying or whining when he was not happy, so much like other parents with louder children, we let him do things the first child was not allowed to do just to keep him quiet, such as wearing cowboy boots with a summer shorts outfit in public. When Andy protested, I told him, "We will just pretend he's the neighbor's kid." Andy liked that.

Periodically, I would ask for help: "Give me strength, Lord." I guess I did it quite often, and Matt knew the protocol. One day, as I was trying to keep calm and deal with a situation, Matt was close by. I took a deep breath, looked up to Heaven, and before I could speak, Matt prayed for me in his little baby voice: "Give 'er stwegth, Lowd." The stress disappeared, I had to laugh.

We were changing our church membership in 1984 when Donald accepted a position as music leader. He and I had agreed on the decision, but I was so uncomfortable the Sunday morning we were to join this new church. I knew this was my opportunity to be rebaptized. The urging from the Holy Spirit had never left me, and it was stronger now. Before we got out of the car, I poured my heart out to Donald. I told him how I had felt the Holy Spirit urging me since I was twelve years old to be rebaptized. It was miserable to talk about it, because I was private about my feelings. I quickly ran through the details to get everything out, took a breath and waited. *There, I did it...what a relief.* The words were out. I'd voiced my nearly lifelong fears of being rebaptized to my husband.

Donald was very understanding. He nodded matter-of-factly and agreed that I should be rebaptized. His reaction was exactly what I needed—no drama and no questions, just acceptance.

We joined the church at the end of the service. The minister, being a friend of ours, was surprised when I told him I wanted to be baptized. Peace poured over me when I made my decision public. It was wonderful! I was finally obedient. The lies and fear of the enemy had held me back.

Somewhere in my religious mind-set, being baptized again was not allowed. People who knew me were a little surprised. My baptism at twelve years old was to please people. Now, my baptism was to truly follow God.

The joy in me that day was evident. While we were shooting a game of pool at his parents' house, following Sunday dinner, Donald told me, "You have really done the right thing today. You're so happy and peaceful." It was more noticeable than I knew. Through that obedient act, God put an extraordinary love in me for people that I had not known. It was instantaneous. I loved people on the street, of all ages and all groups. The doubt concerning my relationship with God was removed and I had peace.

Matt was about five years old, when he was playing in the boys' backyard fort and fell out of the trapdoor. Falling about six feet and landing flat on his back, he was looking up at Andy when I came running out of the house in response to a bloodcurdling scream. It was Andy, sticking his head out through the door in the fort's floor, screaming. Matt lay flat on his back, looking up at Andy. As I was rushing to check him out, Matt pulled himself up and went back to playing. Andy's compassion ran deep and did not want Matt to be hurt.

Through each season, each year, I stayed in prayer and sought God's wisdom on how to work with each of their personalities. My voice tone, words of guidance, and even my approach was tailored to each boy individually.

I fought battles with teachers and school personnel, unknown to Andy, to make them aware of his sensitivity. If he had known, he would have been embarrassed. I kept my eyes and ears open to his reactions and comments each day as he came home from school, a friend's house, or any social gathering to know if something had upset him, while conscious to keep my attention divided equally between both boys. I wanted neither child to feel neglected or second-best. Enjoying my children was also important to me. These years would go quickly. I wanted to have fun and make good memories, so I asked God for these also. His grace is always available for good things.

Chapter 3

Grace to Seek Him

On a Sunday morning, Donald's sister, Brenda, was on her way to church when she was hit by a semi-truck that ran a red light. She had an eight-month-old baby, Blake, whom I'd helped take care of since he was a week old. There had never been a tragedy of this magnitude that hit so close to home.

As Brenda lay in a coma for two weeks, I begged God to let her live. People all over our town were praying. As soon as I hung up the phone, it began ringing again. Many concerned people were calling to check on her condition and find out how they could help. I was stopped in stores, even by people I did not know, to tell me they were praying and to ask about her. If I walked into my yard, people driving by would pull over and ask about Brenda. We had so many calls, I left updated messages on the telephone answering machine regarding her condition.

I was sure she would live. Even if I did not have enough faith, surely all these other people praying for her would. I felt helpless as I took care of my own two boys as well as

Blake. When it was announced by the doctors that Brenda was brain-dead and the decision was made to remove life support, I could not have been more stunned. Back home, away from the hospital and all the people, I told God that He had blown it. If He had healed Brenda, He would have gotten all the praise. This was not a very smart move on His part.

For the next few weeks, I mostly kept to myself in the house with the three boys and conversed only with family, especially my mother-in-law and father-in-law. I felt I could not do enough for them. I knew that if I ever lost a child, my ability to function, even in the smallest tasks, would cease. I was sure something as simple as being able to button a shirt would become impossible.

I was angry with God, and I knew it was wrong. I would tell Him how angry I was...but in the same sentence ask Him to please forgive me and help me understand. I knew He did all things perfectly, and anyway, who else had all the answers? No one. I did not want to become bitter. I had to seek Him. Gradually, His Spirit taught me that He was in control. My faith had to be in Him no matter what the outcome. The Lord spoke to me, something like this, *"You have had a 'Peter Pan' faith. You thought that if you prayed hard enough, believed, and sprinkled some 'pixie dust' that everything would turn out the way you wanted. Can you still trust Me when it does not?"*

I had the misconception that we had been spared from tragedies because we were a strong Christian family. I was in for a very rude awakening; the years ahead were training ground. I had much more to learn. God teaches through adversity, and through Brenda's death, I learned to trust God, regardless of circumstances. By His gentle love, He guided me into truth. I was beginning to see grace in His sovereignty.

Hearing God speak, especially in tragic situations, brings peace. His presence and His voice stills the soul that is crying out for answers.

> "Be careful (*anxious*) for nothing; but in every thing by prayer and supplication with thanksgiving let your requests be made known unto God. And the peace of God that passeth all understanding shall keep your hearts and minds through Christ Jesus." Philippians 4:6–7 (italicized paraphrase—mine)

In 1 Kings, chapter 19, the prophet Elijah sought God in His terrifying moment of being threatened with death from the evil queen Jezebel. Elijah waited alone in the wilderness to hear from God. He was led to Mount Horeb, the mountain of God. God asked Elijah, "What are you doing here?" Elijah, feeling dejected and treated unfairly, told God, "I have been very zealous for the Lord God Almighty. The Israelites have rejected your covenant, torn down your altars, and killed your prophets. I am the only one left, and now they are trying to kill me too." God gave Elijah instructions to go back the way he came and anoint others to help fight the battle. God let Elijah know that he was not the only one serving God; there were 7,000 more who had not worshipped the idols.

Our perception is usually a little off when we try to figure out why God is doing something we do not understand. God will always show us a way out of our despair if we ask Him and are willing to follow His guidance.

We are not exempt from difficult things happening to us just because we are devoted Christians. If we will acknowledge Him, seek wisdom from God, and embrace His truth, we will grow and become more like Him. We will receive instruction for how to live this life. We are not alone. Many are seeking answers. As we come together, we too will be led to the mountain of God, the higher place of His love, truth, and grace. He will even bring something good out of the tragedy if we let Him!

Chapter 4

Grace

"Christ is become of no effect unto you, who-
soever of you are justified by the law; ye are
fallen from grace." Galatians 5:4

Many people think that "fallen from grace" means that they have sinned. According to this verse, Apostle Paul was trying to stop the mind-set that religious acts save us. He was telling the church to remain free from dead rituals and works, knowing that Christ has saved us from sin by the work of the cross. It is the free gift of God's grace that saved us. What caused the Galatians to fall from grace was not sin. It was believing that receiving Jesus Christ as their Savior and that His supreme sacrifice was not enough to cleanse all sin. Thinking that we must do something else to be saved, made the blood of Jesus null and void. If He did not cleanse us from all sin, then He did not cleanse us from any sin. The Galatians were in bondage to a ritual.

"For by grace are ye saved through faith; and
that not of yourselves: it is the gift of God:
Not of works, lest any man should boast."
Ephesians 2:8–9

Everything else we have that is good is also a gift from God and not of ourselves. God spoke to me on this subject, *"Whatever you know or have is by grace."* In other words, I was not to be prideful in any knowledge, visions, or understanding because it was not something I had accomplished myself, but it was by His gift of grace.

God's grace saves us when we receive the blood of Jesus as our payment for sin through faith. When we sin, repent and turn to God, we fall into the arms of Grace not out of them. So much love and so much mercy resides there. If we understand that we can do nothing to save ourselves and trust in the only One who can, our Lord and Savior Jesus Christ, grace will always be there for us.

As I entered church one Sunday morning, feeling like my sins were too great to be forgiven, I saw that the Lord's Supper was set up to be observed that day. Before church could begin, I went straight to the ladies' room to pray. Thank God no one was in there. I told God I knew I was not worthy to participate in the Communion. I wanted Him to reveal to me what I should do. I would participate if that was what he wanted. His Holy Spirit spoke so quietly, *"You are not accepting my forgiveness."* I was elated, but I had to make sure it was Him.

I asked, "Lord, was that you or just me thinking what I wanted to hear?" He spoke stronger this time, *"You are not accepting my forgiveness."* Peace flooded into me.

I felt a hundred pounds lighter. I knew God loved me. I went back to the sanctuary and sat down on the pew. As I looked up toward the pulpit, God gave me a vision as the front of the church seemed to fade away. In its place was a long table. Jesus was seated at the head, and saints from the Bible were seated along both sides. One small, wooden chair was empty and slightly pulled out from the table. I saw myself over to the side. As I stood looking at the chair, I felt an overwhelming presence of acceptance and love. It surrounded me like a blanket. It was so real I could almost touch it. The feeling was like I had never done anything wrong. Not even the presence of forgiveness was there, only pure acceptance and love. There was no indication of any remembrance of sin. The chair was for me, and all I had to do was accept it.

Suddenly, the vision disappeared, and the front of the church came back into view. The altar table was spread with a white linen tablecloth and the brass serving plates were filled with the elements for Communion. I was so excited, I started to turn to the person next to me and ask if they had seen what I had just experienced. Immediately, I realized that was probably not a very good idea since no one else seemed to be nearly as excited. I tried to calm down, which was difficult since I was overwhelmed with joy and elation. I managed to sit back in the pew. I chose to accept God's forgiveness, the symbol of the chair being pulled out for me, and I took Communion that day with renewed faith. God is faithful and just to forgive us of our sins when we ask, and it is as if they never happened. He does not remember it, so why should we? His great grace, through the blood of Jesus, has washed away all our sins.

Grace Harbor

While listening to a program on Christian television one afternoon, the host was interviewing his guest. He asked his guest, "What is grace?" My ears perked up. I was seeking the full meaning of grace. I watched the two men closely and moved a little closer to the TV to be sure to hear all he had to say, but just as the man opened his mouth to speak, his voice went silent. The Holy Spirit had blocked me from hearing the answer. At that precise moment, God began to speak to my spirit, *"Grace is whatever you need at the time that you need it."* Wow! In all my searching, I had not found it explained so fully. I had learned that grace was unmerited favor and forgiveness for sins. It is those things and so much more. When God told Paul that His grace was sufficient for all that he needed, God was giving Paul the answer for every situation—grace. Whatever Paul needed, he had grace for it. When we humble ourselves to ask for God's help, He gives us grace.

Chapter 5

Grace to Overcome the Enemy

In the fall of 1990, Donald's sister's son, Blake, was given over to his father by court order. I missed him so much and had to fight back tears every day. I had helped Donald's parents care for him for almost two years. He was like Andy and Matt's little brother.

One morning, my sister, Tricia, called and told me she was signing up for nursing school at our community college and wanted me to join her. I said, "No." She said, "Fine. Sit around and cry about Blake all day." It sounded like a challenge to me, so I took her up on it and started back to college.

I was taking prerequisites and planned to keep very much to myself. I told God I would not witness to anyone about Him. Knowing God had cleansed and forgiven me did not give me a permit to act like someone who knew Him, I thought. I was feeling worthless and inadequate from past failure. Of course, that is not the way God saw things. It was like the Holy Spirit said, "Great! Now that you've stopped trying to do it yourself, I will work through you."

I was in the library one afternoon, trying to finish a report at the last minute, as usual. A tall, slender young man with long, dark hair, and wearing a tie-died T-shirt, turned in his seat and began talking to me. He was in my anatomy class, and after asking some questions about our assignment, he began pouring out his life's story. His conversation was full of profanity and his immoral lifestyle. Something in me said, "*Have compassion.*" So, I listened politely. He finished, thanked me for listening to him, and left the library in time for me to complete my report.

At times, I would see this young man in the library and around campus. He would tell me of his interest in the New Age movement. I refused to say anything about my faith. I thought to myself, "Fine. Whatever you want to do. Your life is not my business. I'm not saying a word." I did notice that he began cleaning up his language until one day he apologized for letting a curse word "slip out." I had never mentioned a word about his profanity.

After we had a short conversation in the library, he asked me what I believed about God. I said as little as possible: "I believe in Him." Before I left, he had asked so many questions that I ended up giving my testimony, going through the "Roman Road scriptures" of salvation, and pouring out just about all the truth of God I knew. As I left the library, I thought sarcastically, "Thanks a lot, God. You knew how I felt about witnessing." Suddenly, I understood. While I had been answering questions and sharing my faith, the words had come so easily. God had done all of it, not me. I did not have to try. I laughed to myself as I realized He had witnessed through me. His grace was abundant. Joy filled me as I walked to my next class.

Unworthiness, guilt, shame, and failure are all darts of the enemy, Satan, to torment us and stop us from being what God made us. If we agree with the bombardment of the enemy's arsenal of lies he is firing against us, then there we are—stuck in the pit of pathetic-ness (I think I made that word up). None of us are worthy to live in relationship with an ultra-holy God, hence the blood of Jesus was shed for us. It is by grace through that blood that we are called to come to His Throne of Grace, without hesitation, running with joy, exuberant and full of confidence that our Father loves us and will gladly receive us.

Not only does God want us to get out of the pit, He wants us to be exalted above the enemy that deceived us.

> "And now shall mine head be lifted up above
> mine enemies round about me: therefore,
> will I offer in his tabernacle sacrifices of joy;
> I will sing, yea, I will sing praises unto the
> Lord." Psalms 27:6

The real enemy is Satan sending his condemning words into our thoughts, and when we agree with those negative thoughts, we are sunk. Without knowing it, some people are used by Satan to carry out his plans against us, saying his words and making us feel worse. When we let God fight our battles for us, we win big. We stay covered in grace and surrounded with favor.

After many long nights of studying, I finished nursing school. Sometimes, I had brought my study group home after classes so I would be available to the boys when they came home from school, but most of my studying was done at night so my days were given to Andy and Matt. There was so much conflict among the students with backstabbing and malicious gossip. They missed no one, including me. I had kept to myself, except for three women God had given me, with whom I studied those last two years. Some criticized because our study group was multicultural. Others thought there was favoritism from the instructors.

When it came time for graduation, I was surprised to be recognized for an award of high achievement. A nursing instructor told Donald it was the highest honor of achievement for nursing. Standing on the platform while receiving the award (with a pounding headache), the Holy Spirit spoke to my heart: *"I am preparing a table before you in the presence of your enemies."* I had not understood that verse very well from the twenty-third Psalm, but now I did. God had chosen for me to receive this award as my defense:

> "Thou preparest a table before me in the
> presence of mine enemies: thou anointest
> my head with oil; my cup runneth over."
> Psalm 23:5

It was more than I could have imagined. God had honored me in front of my enemies, this time, it was the people the devil had used. This was surely the grace of God and I was being surrounded with favor as with a shield.

> "For Thou, LORD, wilt bless the righteous;
> with favor wilt Thou compass him as with a
> shield." Psalms 5:12

We can let God take care of those who oppose us. He knows our hearts and theirs. He knows what will protect us and what will deliver those who are being used by Satan to hurt us. We can pray for them and even minister through love by not retaliating. God's grace lifts our head above the enemy's attacks. He uses the attacks to exalt those who trust Him. There is none so good as Him!

Chapter 6

Andy

On April 5, 1996, we were watching our thirteen-year-old son, Matt, play baseball at the Southside Baseball Complex in Lake City, Florida. My husband, Donald, and I sat in our lawn chairs laughing and talking. I looked up and saw a STAT flight emergency helicopter overhead leaving Lake City. I said, "I hate to see those things." Minutes later, one of the ballplayer's father, a Florida highway patrolman, came walking into the park. We thought nothing about it since his son played on our son's team. He came up to us and asked for Donald to come talk to him. A few seconds later, something made me jump out of my chair and rush to hear what he was saying.

Donald spoke loud and firm to me: "Get Matt! Andy's been in an accident!" That was all we were told. Our sixteen-year-old son, Andy, had been out of town at a mall with his friends. I had not worried about him all day, which was very unusual for me.

I rushed to the dugout, called for Matt, and started running to catch up with Donald and the trooper. Suddenly, in my spirit, I heard the words *"He's dead."* Energy drained from my body. My legs went limp. I saw the ground and knew I was about to hit it face-first. I did not have the strength to put my hands in front of me to try and break the fall. I felt someone take my hand. It was the wife of another trooper with whom I had worked at the Florida Highway Patrol years ago. Her son was playing on the opposing team. She pulled me by the hand and yelled, "Dawn, come on!"

I whispered, "He's dead," being too weak to vocalize words.

She spoke strongly to me: "You've got to go with your family!" She had grabbed our abandoned lawn chairs and was carrying them under one arm while pulling my hand with her free one. One foot stumbled in front of the other as I felt her urgency to get me to the parking lot with Donald, Matt, and the trooper. I was too weak to walk. Breathing was an effort. Once again, I heard the Voice. It was nothing profound or very spiritual. He said, *"It's okay."*

Immediately, energy poured back into my body like Heaven had opened over me. Strength and excitement shot into every portion of my being. I came alive! I had to tell Donald. I knew if God was telling me it was okay, then every-thing was all right. Mostly, I knew we were not alone; God had this. I started running. When I caught up with Donald, Matt, and the trooper standing by our car, I looked behind me and thanked the woman who had helped me get to the car. I turned to Donald and blurted out, "Andy's dead, but it's okay!" I was excited! How strange. Donald, Matt, and the trooper all turned to look at me, their mouths slightly open as if they had stopped talking in midsentence. The expres-sion on the faces of Donald and the trooper was as if they were momentarily frozen, unable to comprehend some for-eign language I had just spoken. I realized it would be better if I did not say anything else. I was much too joyful, and it did not make sense.

Donald shouted, "Andy's fine! He's at the house!" I knew Andy was not at home. I knew the truth, but at that moment, those words had been given to me by the Holy Spirit and it would not be truth or comfort unless God Himself revealed it to others. I asked the trooper where we were going. He said, "To your house." I felt that if Andy was not in the hospital or Highway Patrol station, he was gone.

I rode in the back seat of the car in silence. Matt was in the front passenger's seat, while Donald followed the trooper to our home, both driving furiously. As we pulled into our driveway, I saw that another trooper was there and so was Donald's dad, waiting for us outside the house. Donald's dad was crying. As we jumped out of the car, he spoke through broken sobs, "Andy's dead."

The trooper who came to get us and happened to be the son of the lieutenant I had worked for years ago at the Florida Highway Patrol, gave us some details of the accident and read the suicide note. With each detail, I felt a stabbing pain in my stomach. When the note was read, it was all just a blur, but I heard enough to know it was just like Andy, condemning himself and feeling worthless. I had worked to battle Andy's low self-esteem since preschool. He had been a precious, compassionate, obedient child who was a joy to raise. Many people had commented that they would like their child, grandchild, or other students to be just like him. He never saw this. Mostly, he only saw what he perceived to be negativity in his own life. I had felt Andy could have been suicidal in grade school and I begged God to show him, in some way, that he was liked and cared about. He was in the fourth grade at that time and was voted vice president of his school. What an answer to my prayer! It seemed to help for a time, but it was a short-lived victory. Soon, he was back in the battle. I had talked with counselors, friends, and other parents, but no one could see the problem because he was so good and so smart that he kept it well hidden, even from a very young age. He knew what behavior was expected and portrayed it well.

I had thought I needed to keep building him up, praying for him, encouraging him, and involving him in various sports activities and especially church. I was doing everything I knew to build his confidence. Prayer was continuous.

A few weeks before the accident, I remembered telling God, "I know what it means to pray without ceasing." It seemed I was praying constantly for Andy, late into the night and early hours of the morning. I knew he was struggling. He had been changing for a while. I ignored his outbursts of anger.

About three weeks before the accident, I received a phone call from a friend who had been a real blessing through the years. There were three of us God had put together for this time and purpose. We three shared a special bond. Denise, one of the three, called to tell me that Patti, the third partner in our prayer triangle, had tried to call but did not reach me. Patti had been praying when God gave her an urgency to pray for me. This was not the first time this had happened. The Lord conveyed to her that she was to give me the following message from Him:

"He loves you."

"He has heard your prayers."

"His arms are around your family."

"His hand is unchanging."

Denise asked, "What have you been praying for?"

I answered, "My kids. It's always my kids."

When we got together a couple days later, all three of us tried to decipher the message. That part about the unchanging hand had us a little confused. I told the others that all I knew was that something was going to happen, but I did not know what. I laughed a little when I said, "God doesn't drop by just to say 'Hello!'" I knew He had purpose in everything He did. I felt no fear.

When the trooper finished talking with us, I felt a little nauseous and was in a deep reflective state. I had nothing to say. The wheels in my mind were turning. I knew in my heart that Andy was in Heaven; his mental pain and anguish were over. The battle was ended. I was not in tune, so much, with all that was going on around me; my spirit remained open to hear from Heaven. I had peace.

The trooper who had come to the baseball field walked us to the front door. Tears were in his eyes as he offered his help in any way. There was such compassion on his face. I hugged him and thanked him for all he had done. I later learned that he and his wife drove past our house until two a.m., just to make sure we were not alone and that everything was all right. What compassion.

Neighbors came out of their houses to comfort us. Someone asked, "Who do we need to call?"

It was hard to concentrate. My parents needed to be told. I questioned myself, "Who could tell them?" Then I thought of Shirley, a good friend for twenty years, who lived near my parents. She had helped direct my wedding, had hosted my baby shower, had helped me when we worked together at the Department of Transportation, and had been so much more than just a friend. God had brought her into my life. We often knew what the other was thinking without words being said. Now, I was asking her to do one of the most difficult things ever—tell my parents their first grandchild was dead. I gave my neighbor the phone number, knowing Shirley would take care of this difficult task.

Compassionately, I was asked by a neighbor, "What about your pastor?" Yes! I wanted Elmer and Nancy called right away. The people at my church understood the sovereignty of God and would know that He was still in control of even this situation. I wanted them with us.

People began pouring into our home. Soon there was standing room only, and even that was scarce. Cars were parked all over the yard and down the street. I kept hearing myself telling people, "It's okay." There was so much meaning in those words that had given strength back into my body earlier. I knew in my heart that was the comfort God had given me to keep me from going into shock. His Holy Spirit had poured out in me great strength and joy from Heaven, because from Heaven's perspective everything was okay. Andy was in Heaven; what place could be better? As horrible as the incident appeared, the outcome was okay; in fact, from God's point of view, it was very good! God gave me His perspective and took away my own so that I could see the other side of the situation, His side, and that is always better than ours.

People continued flooding into our home. As Donald relayed the incident and told about Andy's life, one man commented, "It surely must have been God's will." His wife quickly reprimanded him. I told her, "That is exactly right! This is God's will." Somehow it excited me for someone else to see it, even though I did not understand it all myself.

The love and care shown to us was so much comfort. I would never have thought so many people would have cared about us. At one point, I was sitting in a chair in our den with Matt. As I looked out into the room, I saw that women were seated on the floor all around me from wall to wall. I felt so much love from these precious ladies, as one by one they would come to hug me and give words of comfort and encouragement.

Sometime after two a.m., everyone had gone except for my sister Tricia and my close friend Shirley. They encouraged me to get cleaned up and thought that a shower would help refresh me. I told them I really did not want to be alone. The thought of handling this without people constantly hugging me and speaking words of comfort every minute was a little scary. They promised to sit outside the bathroom door and yell to me in the shower. We laughed, and I went to my bedroom to get ready.

Being alone, I allowed myself to think back over the day. I cried out to the Lord in my spirit, "God, You said You heard my prayers." His Spirit spoke quietly to me, "*You prayed for Andy to have peace and joy, and now he does.*" My anguish subsided, once again, I was filled with peace. This, of course, was not the way I had wanted it, but somehow God was in all of this. Andy was such a perfectionist; now he had perfect peace, perfect joy, perfect love. No one could hurt him again. He was in the arms of Jesus. Andy, being intelligent and deep, had trouble finding answers to all his questions; now he knew the answers. Now he was perfect.

As I was alone, the Lord poured His words into my spirit: "*This is the way it is supposed to be. Andy came here to live for this time period only. You, Donald, and Matt will go on for a little while together, but not for long, then you will be reunited. My hand is unchanging.*" There were the words He had spoken to Patti during her prayer time: "My hand is unchanging." Now I understood. This would come to pass no matter what I did or did not do. God was in control, not me.

I thought back to four months earlier, when I'd had an uneasiness at work. I felt I had to call the high school and make sure Andy was there, but I got busy working with my own students at the ninth-grade school, where I doubled as the nurse and a teacher. An hour later, there was the uneasiness again. I called the school. Andy was not there. I panicked. I did not believe Andy would skip school. I raced home. Donald happened to be there in the studio. I told him Andy was missing. We looked for him for two hours. A lengthy note had been left on his desk; he wrote with such depth I could not understand it. I had carried the note with us as we looked for him along the roadside and at various places he frequented. I called friends he knew as we searched.

After the two-hour search, I told God that Andy was in His hands (like I really had to tell Him) and I felt a peace as I laid the note back on Andy's desk. Suddenly, I heard a noise from Andy's closet. As I opened the door, I saw Andy lying on the floor. I fell on him and cried. I told him I loved him and was so afraid I would never see him again. He then told me he had taken a handful of Tylenol. I called for Donald to help him to the car to go to the hospital. I became angry because I could not understand this action, but God showed me Andy needed my love and acceptance.

God had spared Andy's life that day. He could do it again if He chose, but He did not choose. Thirty minutes before Andy died, he had called me on the car phone to tell me he was back from the mall and did not want me to worry about him. He was going to a friend's house and he loved me. I told him I was not worried and that I loved him too. I had such peace. Andy sounded as though he had been having a good time with his friends. Later, my mother reminded me I had talked to her that morning about Andy going with his friends and had told her that I had put him in God's hands. That is the only way I can explain the peace I had all that day, because I was a natural-born worrier.

That night, the Lord's voice consumed all my thoughts. He said, "*I am going to bless your family.*" Great emphasis was placed on the word "bless." It was good to hear, even though I could not comprehend what all that really meant. I just knew I did not want this peace I had, nor my sound mind, to leave.

God continued pouring out His Spirit, showing me He had given the best to Andy in Heaven. The day of the funeral, while I was talking to our pastor's wife in our living room, the Holy Spirit began speaking to me again. I stopped talking and told her the Lord was speaking to me as I closed my eyes to focus on Him. I knew this was not a common occurrence for people in our church, but it was natural to me and at this point, all my inhibitions concerning the Lord were gone. I even relayed to my pastor's wife the words He spoke to me. He said, "*All you have tried to do for Andy* (to make him feel good about himself and make him happy), *I am now doing and doing it perfectly.*" As these words were being spoken to me, I received a vision of Andy. His head was laying on Jesus's chest and, though I could only see his back, he looked exhausted. Jesus was sitting and had a big smile on his face. His arms were around Andy. I no longer had to worry about Andy; Jesus was taking good care of him. I had told a pastor's wife, when Andy was much younger, that I always felt I would lose him one day. Now the words of Job resounded in my mind:

> "For the thing which I greatly feared is come
> upon me, and that which I was afraid of is
> come unto me." Job 3:25

Yet, here was God, surrounding me with His love and comforting my spirit. He was giving me the peace that passes all understanding. I was amazed at my ability to think so clearly. A few days later, I received another vision of Andy. He was bigger than life and he was radiating with joy. A light was all around him and his expression was jubilant! This vision appeared to me multiple times a day for probably about a year. It was God's way to help remove grief and remind me that Andy's latter state was greater than his former.

The grace that wrapped me up that day was beyond anything that I can explain. The Bible states:

> "Grace and peace be multiplied unto you
> through the knowledge of God, and of Jesus
> our Lord." 2 Peter 1:2

It seemed I had been seeking to know God from a child, reading the Bible and Bible storybooks, desiring to be in church and Sunday School classes. Seeking the knowledge of God had multiplied grace and peace to me in the time I needed it most.

I believe that the more understanding we have of who God is, through His Word, the more grace we are capable of receiving. We trust Him and His Word to be true, to a greater extent, the better we get to know Him. So many times, we brush off the grace being given to us, believing that He cannot be as good as He is, or that we do not deserve it .

Thoughts of others who went through tragedy and suffered tremendously tried to tell me I did not deserve to have so much joy. The Holy Spirit would bring to my remembrance scripture that told me truth, refuting the lies of my carnal thinking or lies from the enemy. We read:

> "But I would not have you to be ignorant, brethren, concerning them which are asleep, that ye sorrow not, even as others which have no hope. For if we believe that Jesus died and rose again, even so them also which sleep in Jesus will God bring with him."
> 1Thessalonians 4:13–14

There is a blessed hope within us that keeps us looking up, if we choose it. I had to make the choice every day to receive God's words, visions, and truth over the world's expectations, lies, and human nature. God gave me grace to choose truth and joy.

Chapter 7

Sustaining Grace

I was wrapped up in grace like being snuggled in a cocoon. Nothing, not even some of the harsh words spoken by others, seemed to penetrate the grace that was given to me. Like with Job and his friends, who were not the most comforting in his trials, some people did not have the most encouraging things to say. God's grace kept me in peace and made me aware of how much they did not understand God's ways and that I was only learning.

> "For my thoughts are not your thoughts, nei-
> ther are your ways my ways, saith the LORD."
> Isaiah 55:8

I wanted to hear His thoughts and I wanted to hear His voice. Even though we do not understand the ways of God, He promises to give us peace through it all. I knew His peace would keep me sane:

"Thou wilt keep him in perfect peace, whose
   mind is stayed on Thee: because he trusteth
   in Thee." Isaiah 26:3

In one of my prayer times, years earlier, I had asked God
to teach me about His grace. I did not realize I would get
hands-on training. I only wanted a little more Bible study
on the subject, not a collision course with destiny, but as
the Bible says:

"He gives us exceedingly abundantly more
   than we can ask or think." Ephesians 3:20

In the days ahead following Andy's promotion to Heaven,
God constantly filled me with His love and grace. It seemed
He was always teaching me. The Holy Spirit brought back
to my mind an experience with Him I had about ten years
prior. I had been pulling a thick blanket, or comforter, over
me as I was getting ready to go to sleep. The words dropped
into my mind, "*The Holy Spirit is the Comforter and, like this
blanket, surrounds you and shelters you from the harshness
of the outside world.*" His Holy Spirit, the Comforter, was
sheltering us, protecting us, wrapping Himself around us
and teaching us all things. He was protecting us from things
people said that were not of God. He was also protecting us
from falling into devastating grief. Beautifully and simply,
God portrayed His truth. I praised Him for this reminder.
What a beautiful picture of the grace of which I had asked
to have more understanding. Grace is protection, as well as
peace and strength. His grace is His overflowing love to us.
   In my spirit, I saw the Lord holding a vast amount of love
in His arms and sprinkling it down on all the people who

came to our home; sent food, flowers, cards, or letters; or called and prayed for us. He had put His love and care into hundreds of people as a way of showing His love. It caused them to be drawn to us. It is His love that we need in us to fulfill His work on this earth, and these people were fulfilling God's love by coming and being with us. God gave His people grace to stop their busy lives and come to comfort us. How wonderful is our Lord, overflowing with compassion and mercy. This vision caused me to realize the important role we play when we take part in someone's life. God was turning people to us to carry His comfort.

We are His hands and feet. We are His ministers when we bring food, send a card, give a hug, or just sit quietly with a friend who needs support.

A couple days before Andy's service, I was sitting in my living room, with people all around. A woman took my hand as she looked down at me. She was so heavy-hearted as she recalled Andy's intelligence and gifts as a musician. She sobbed, "What a waste."

Immediately, the words leapt into my mind: *"Not wasted—perfected."* Joy consumed me. In the presence of God, all is perfected. I did not attempt to explain to her what the Holy Spirit had just revealed to me. The joy I was feeling could not be explained. I smiled up at her and squeezed her hand. She probably thought I was taking some very good drugs. I do not remember her face or who she was, but God used her, as she felt compassion and grief for our family, to make known to me another one of His truths.

In Heaven, Andy did not lose his ability to play music on the instruments he loved. He was using that talent and skill with perfection. Everything that Andy enjoyed here, he was doing in Heaven with more joy and greater ability. God's words reminded me of the vision I was seeing daily with his big smile and being full of life. He was having a great time in Heaven!

For days our home was filled with precious, loving people. Food, phone calls, flowers, cards, letters, and hugs arrived in abundance. I looked forward to these contacts and drew strength from them as I acknowledged each as a blessing from God. I fondly remember a church member, Dwight, smiling at me and quietly stating as we sat in our living room, filled with people and conversation, "The Holy Spirit is here." I smiled back at him. I knew the Holy Spirit was in our home, but it was good to hear someone say it.

The morning of the funeral, I prepared myself. I went to my bedroom, away from family and friends, got on my knees, and asked God to give me peace. I immediately felt His supernatural peace flow into me. I was reminded that this service was only a ceremony for those left behind, Andy would not be there. He was not in the casket. He was home. He had eternal life, never to die again, and he was full of joy. God was giving me more grace for the service ahead.

As we drove up to the church, cars were parked everywhere in the streets. The church was filled to overflowing out the doors. We were led in and seated in the front row. The choir loft was filled because there was no other place for people to sit. I could see the faces of people I knew. How sweet of them to come. They encouraged me by their presence. "Blessed Assurance" was sung by a dear friend of ours. What a perfect song Donald had chosen—assurance of God's love and grace. The song and the singer brought more peace.

The first pastor spoke of Andy's baptism and profession of faith, made when he was six years old. This pastor had once told me that Andy had more understanding of accepting Jesus as his Savior at the young age of six than many adults do. He had also asked Andy if he could quote John 3:16. Andy had surprised the pastor by quoting John 3:16 and answering questions with such maturity. He had loved learning about God and memorizing scripture starting at an early age. One of his friends reminded me that Andy had led him to the Lord when they were in seventh grade. God had been as much a part of Andy's life as any other essential. Even as a teenager, when he seemed to be questioning God, I walked in his room to find him kneeling and praying beside his bed. This was a meaningful sight to me as his mother.

The second pastor to speak was Elmer, our pastor from Westside Chapel. He spoke as though his heart was breaking, but his words were determined and his faith in God's sovereignty was strong. This man touched my heart, as he seemed to be feeling our sorrow and carrying our burden. God had surely led us to this church to learn more of His grace.

I had only gone to Westside, about four years previously, to accompany a friend who did not want to go alone. As I walked into the nearly empty sanctuary early that morning to meet her, I heard the words in my spirit, *"You're home."*

I argued back, "This isn't where I belong, I go to another church." I could not deny the feeling of familiarity and comfort even though I had never been there. The truth that was preached kept me coming back, even when no one else went with me. I would go to the early service at Westside and after the service, pick up my family and go to our church. Tears would fill my eyes as the truths that had been revealed to me in my own private Bible study were taught at the Chapel. Before this, I had not heard them taught anywhere else. The Holy Spirit was here, and I was hungry for His teaching. As weeks passed, we joined the Chapel, and there the sovereignty of God was made known to me. Even though I tried to fight against God's complete control, he brought to me His knowledge of the truth. God is working out a plan, a plan for our lives individually and personally. We have choices to make and through the choices we make, good or bad, He will fulfill His purpose through us as His children. I know that I needed this truth to have the peace through which He sustained me. There was purpose in attending this church. The steps I had taken in life were being led by God's sovereign grace.

It had all been in God's plan. His ways were not our ways. His hand was unchanging. He was love to us. All was working out for His purpose and good pleasure. He was not punishing us; He was sparing us from evil. He was pouring out His mercy and grace. His strength had been made perfect in our weakness.

As we walked out of the church following the casket, I did not feel comfortable looking at the hundreds of people around us and in the balcony, but when the procession was held up at the door, I heard my name spoken softly. I turned to see nurses with whom I'd worked in the ICU and one of the doctors that I had chosen to see Andy. They stood by the door because there were no seats left. As they reached out their hands to touch my arm, again I felt God's love flowing through them to me. He is always with us. It was more of God's grace reaching out to us through His people, comforting us.

As the weeks passed, I kept thinking, "I am in shock now, and any day I am going to fall apart." I kept waiting for the big breakdown to come, but it never did. I went through all of Andy's writings, clothes, collections, and home movies, thinking this would bring me to a breaking point and be done with it, but God's Holy Spirit, the Comforter, gave me the peace that passes all understanding and taught me the things He wanted me to know:

> "Do not be anxious *or* worried about anything, but in everything [every circumstance and situation] by prayer and petition with thanksgiving, continue to make your [specific] requests known to God. And the peace of God [that peace which reassures the heart, that peace] which transcends all understanding, [that peace which] stands guard over your hearts and your minds in Christ Jesus [is yours]." Philippians 4:6–7 (Amplified)

He kept me covered in protective grace as I kept reaching out to receive it. When I became overwhelmed with feelings of grief, the Lord brought His truths to my mind.

For example, while driving from work to pick up Matt from school one day, I started crying and then really sobbing. Within seconds, I realized I was singing a song while I was crying. I began listening to my own words, "When the cross seems heavy you are called to bear, count your many blessings..." Once more I was filled with peace. I spoke out loud to God while I was driving, "God, again, You didn't allow me to cry for long, did you?" I knew it was Him giving me the song to comfort me. I had been so blessed and had many blessings to count!

He had taught me truth concerning the Holy Spirit, the Comforter. No one can remove the grief and pain as He can. He empowers His people to carry His love and comfort to others as He did when He walked on earth as a man. How could I complain? The Lord had blessed me so much by showing me that Andy was happy and joyful. He had given me great peace through this storm. He had given me a Christian home that even with our faults and failures we could go forward with hope. He had given us our precious son, Matt, who loved to make us laugh. He had surrounded us with many loving people. He brought us to a place where we could be taught the truth to prepare our hearts for this day. He had not forsaken us; He upheld us with His sustaining grace.

Chapter 8

Grace, Grace, and More Grace

In the first few days, I was reminded of how, in the Bible, Satan asked God for permission to afflict Job. Satan had not oppressed my son without God's permission. The God who loved Andy more than me had allowed for this to be the way He would glorify Himself and further His Kingdom. This gave me comfort, peace, and strength. I saw relationships healed, the lost turned to God, and Christians draw closer to Him through Andy's death. I was not angry at God. He had shown mercy on Andy. Andy felt things deeper than I could have imagined and hurt more often than we knew. Though, I would have gladly given my whole life to loving, comforting, and trying to find new ways to build Andy up, but God chose not to allow that. There are things we will not understand fully in this life. We must trust God; He knows what is best. In the Bible, we read:

"The righteous perisheth, and no man layeth
it to heart: and merciful men are taken away,

none considering that the righteous is taken
away from the evil to come." Isaiah 57:1

Donald, Matt, and I left Lake City a few days after the funeral to visit friends in Lakeland. While we were there, a neighbor, who knew us from Donald having sung at their church, came to see us. She told me she had bought a book a couple of weeks before and now she knew why: it was meant to be given to us. As she handed me the book, I saw it was by an author with whom I was familiar, and all throughout the book proclaimed the sovereignty of God. How like Him! Even miles away from home, God was sending His love and divine message through His people: "I am in control."

I did not know why God chose to teach me these things or to give me such peace in this storm. I deserved to be suffering, as I always knew I would if anything ever happened to one of my children. I was sure He had something to do with my prayer years ago that asked for a better understanding of His grace. I praised Him daily for bringing me out of the devastation and hopelessness I first felt when I heard the words in my spirit, "He's dead." In that state, I knew someone would have had to carry me to the car and I would have been on drugs and under a doctor's care for who knows how long. God could have left me there, but He did not. I was healed from a large portion of my grief when He told me, "It's okay." My spirit came alive from knowing that this was God's will, this was best for this time. His plan cannot be stayed, and we would not want it to be if we knew the whole truth.

God had a reason and He had purpose in His plan. I am so grateful for the years I had with Andy. I felt Andy close to me. He had a great impact on my life with all his knowledge and sensitivity, his humor and wit, and I continue to look forward to that day of our reunion. His life had only been meant for this number of years and no more. He had accomplished all God had for him on this earth. His talents were not wasted—but perfected in the presence of God.

When I would question God or start thinking, "What if…" I was quickly reminded of God's grace toward me and almost ashamed that I could grieve when God had been so good to show me His love.

All that He did for us cannot be written down. Daily, I was seeing His presence made real in our lives. My closest friends stated that they had never seen God's work so evident in anyone's life. They told me that the way I was handling everything was not like me or my personality. I was wrapped up in God's grace like being in a cocoon. Only God could give the peace and joy they saw displayed. Sometimes I could hardly contain the excitement as I saw His Holy Spirit working day by day. I knew that whatever was in store for us, God would be with us. He made us stronger and gave us more power than we ever dreamed. Truly, it was okay.

The apostle wrote:

> "And he said unto me, my grace is sufficient for thee: for my strength is made perfect in weakness…" 2 Corinthians 12:9

God had given grace that was more than sufficient, more than we needed to get through this tough time. He had given an abundance of grace, not just to survive but to thrive. Truly, we had been blessed with grace, grace, and more grace.

Chapter 9

There's a War?

A Bible teacher stated that when things come in threes, she pays more attention, feeling it may be from God. The very month that Andy died, I received a magazine in the mail that carried an article called "Joy Comes in the Morning." I began reading it, not knowing it was about a teenage suicide. The article talked about how the thief comes to steal, kill, and destroy. I really did not understand what it was referring to then, but it stayed in my mind.

A few nights later, I could not sleep. Grief was overwhelming me. Guilt was heavy from things I thought maybe I could have changed in the past. Then the words came to me, *"The thief comes to steal, kill, and destroy."* I suddenly realized that is what was happening to the peace and joy God had given me. Realizing the guilt and pain were coming from Satan, I asked God to restore His peace to me and I went to sleep. A few days later, I received a pamphlet in the mail from my grandmother about grief. I opened it up to the middle and started reading. There, the pamphlet referred to

Satan coming to steal, kill, and destroy God's peace. It was my third encounter with this statement within about a week.

Grief is from the enemy, peace is from God. I had even felt guilty at times for not grieving more. I wondered what was wrong with me. God was supplying the peace and joy. He knew what a treasure my children were to me. He gave me a heart for my children. I thanked Him for the peace He gave me. Satan, along with a few people, had tried to make me doubt Andy's salvation, but God had shown me that Andy had peace, love, and joy and that he was in the arms of Jesus. For me to allow the enemy to steal my joy and gratitude would be participating in Satan's assault on God's goodness.

God's miraculous grace covered me for approximately four months then slowly began to lift, but He was with me. Yes, I missed Andy, and there were tears occasionally, because it would be a while before I would see him again, but God had shown me the spiritual side of this tragedy, and it had an entirely different meaning than what I had seen in the flesh. With my own carnal mind, all I could see was the devastation, loss, and pain. With God, I could see Andy's joy and peace. I could see eternity waiting for us, where there would never be any separation or pain again. I also knew there was purpose and things to accomplish before that time would come.

I started becoming a little fearful as my own inhibitions returned. I ran to God, asking Him not to let me be overwhelmed with grief or sorrow. I did not want to plunge to the depths of despair like I had felt the first few seconds I realized Andy was gone.

I came down to earth, but peace, joy, and grace remained. It was not the mountaintop high I had experienced. I still felt God's love and presence. God gently and slowly lifted the covering that had kept out all the harsh feelings while showing me that He would still be with me. I was stronger because of God's drawing me near to Him and giving me that time to adjust.

It had been difficult to explain such abundant joy, and I tried to avoid contact with those in grief because I felt they could not understand what made me so happy when they were hurting so much. The joy I had those first four months was not natural; it was supernatural, and I attempted to minister more to those hurting by writing notes and cards. I was surprised how many people God sent to me who needed ministry in what should have been my time of need.

During one of the days that I was feeling what I called the "grace covering" lifting, I was on my knees beside my bed, praying, when I was urged in my spirit to *"Put on the whole armor."* I jumped up to get my Bible and turned to Ephesians 6:

> "Finally, my brethren, be strong in the Lord, and in the power of his might. Put on the whole armor of God, that ye may be able to stand against the wiles of the devil. For we wrestle not against flesh and blood, but against principalities, against powers, against the rulers of the darkness of this world, against spiritual wickedness in high places. Wherefore take unto you the whole armor of God, that ye may be able to withstand in the evil day, and having done all, to stand. Stand therefore, having your loins girt about with truth, and having on the breastplate of righteousness;

And your feet shod with the preparation of the gospel of peace; Above all, taking the shield of faith, wherewith ye shall be able to quench all the fiery darts of the wicked. And take the helmet of salvation, and the sword of the Spirit, which is the word of God: Praying always with all prayer and supplication in the Spirit, and watching thereunto with all perseverance and supplication for all saints;"
Ephesians 6:10–18

I did not know what was coming, but I knew I had to prepare and study the scripture. Soon after, our ladies' Sunday School class decided to do a study on spiritual warfare. God is so good. He already had a plan for teaching me about the armor. I poured over the study book and finished it months before the class. I knew I needed it now. I had known, even when I was walking in God's grace, that Satan would not let this miraculous experience go unchallenged. He would have his time of retaliation. Still, I had peace.

I prayed for God to help me understand the armor and to stand firm. I also prayed Ephesians 3:16:

"That He would grant you, according to the riches of His glory, to be strengthened with might by His Spirit in the inner man,"
Ephesians 3:16

I inserted each family member's name to be strengthened by the might of the Holy Spirit in the inner man. I immediately wrote the names of my family in my

Bible beside the verse. Praying scripture is praying God's perfect will.

The attacks came. Satan hit hard and continuously. Shortly after the funeral, Donald began to be less and less present at home. He did not talk much. Because of the uncommon peace and joy God had given me, I knew that if I said too much, it would be offensive to him; he did not understand my reaction. One night, Matt asked me where Dad was. Doing everything I knew to keep any more drama out of our house, I calmly and casually said, "Dad had to work." I did not know where Donald was, but I thought that he was probably hanging out at his work. Desperately, I was calling out to God for Donald to have peace and for us to be able to talk.

A few days later, Donald had an experience with God when the car he was driving broke down on the side of the road.

As he lifted the hood, God spoke to him, "*Like this battery has no power without being connected to the alternator, so do you have no power not being connected to me.*"

Donald came home and told me of the encounter. I was overjoyed. He told how he had been running from God and me because he could see God was with me. He had also been suicidal, wanting to kill himself, even driving at crazy high speeds on dangerous roads. It was like the spirit of suicide that had been on Andy jumped onto Donald. Through my desperate prayers and God's mercy, Donald's life had been preserved and his eyes were opened. Thank God! Satan looks for people to devour. Donald's hurt and anger pushed God away, opening the door for other things.

I had never been one to talk about spiritual warfare; I had never known much about it. I had heard a minister say that some people get carried away and think there is a demon behind every rock. I had not wanted to be one of *those* people, but I was beginning to feel there were ten demons behind every rock. God allowed me to see that the same spirit that attacked Andy was attacking our family again. I was not afraid. I went to God in prayer and reading scripture again and again. His word removes fear, as truth is planted in the soul and replaces the lies of the enemy. God is our fortress. He is the safe harbor of grace. I was praying with all that was within me for God to release our family from this bondage of attacks.

It was amazing to me how I felt such love for the ones Satan was using because I knew the enemy was not those people. The battle was not against the flesh and blood; it was spiritual. Attacks came from every direction. Yet, it seemed so appropriate; Satan was still fighting to destroy our family as God had shown me he would try to do. Each battle ended with the Lord being victorious. Each battle brought a deeper knowledge of God's love. From the beginning of all these events, it had been a spiritual awakening for me. One attack that seemed very trivial compared to the others released me from more guilt.

Upon arriving at work one morning at the ninth-grade high school, where I was the nurse and medical skills teacher, I opened the door to the clinic and saw, written on the sign on the door next to my name, the words—SON KILLER. I ripped the sign off the door and, sobbing, went straight to one of the office staff, who was my friend. I laid it on her desk, crying so hard I was unable to speak.

She sighed heavily as she put her arms around me. "Dawn," she said; then, stomping her foot hard on the floor, she raised her voice. "This is from Satan! We are not going to let him win!"

I knew that! Why was I crying so hard? Why couldn't I brush this off? The whole school had been vandalized. What was wrong with me that I could not give this to God like all the other attacks? They had been so much worse. The more I tried to stop crying, the worse it got. I had not cried this much over Andy. I had to go home.

When I walked in my back door, I went straight to my sofa, where I met God for my early morning devotions, and fell on my knees. I cried out to Him, "What is wrong with me? I know who this is coming from; why can't I release it to you, Lord?" I do not know how long I stayed on my knees praying and crying; I had no concept of time.

Finally, I was able to get up. I was physically exhausted. I had no answers, but at least I had stopped crying. I needed to sleep, which was sort of strange for that time of day, but I felt so drained.

When I woke up, there were still several hours of school remaining. I felt determined not to let Satan keep me down. I went back to work. The news had spread through the faculty and staff about the cruel words written on my door. Many came to speak words of comfort and encouragement to me. Some told me not to let things bother me so much. I wanted to say something sarcastic, but I just smiled. What a wimp! Where was my strong Christian faith?

I stayed in constant prayer as I worked. As the hours went by, God began revealing to me the reason for my weakness. He spoke to my spirit, *"You believed the words 'son killer' were true."*

I had listened to rumors from other people and guilty thoughts that ran through my mind and instead of dismissing them, I dwelt on them. God had revealed to me that I was not under condemnation, but I held on to the guilt. Satan was able to attack me in this area because of my unbelief.

God was right. When people asked, "What was wrong with the parents?" I had asked the same question. Yes, we made mistakes, as all parents do, but God had shown me over and over this was not our guilt to carry. Instantly, I asked God to help me release the guilt and give it to Him. Another step in God's direction had been made. The attack that should have been the most insignificant had taught me that disobedience or lack of faith opens the door for Satan to gain a stronghold. My mind had to agree with God and His word, especially about myself, to win every battle. The choice was mine to make—agree with Satan, who accuses and condemns, or agree with God, the giver of all truth. I had to make a choice:

> "... I have set before you life and death, blessing and cursing: therefore choose life, that both thou and thy seed may live:"
> Deuteronomy 30:19

God's word is life. If we choose what He says, we shall live in abundance. Satan is an accuser of those in the body of Christ. His words bring death—death to our spirit, death to our soul, death to our joy and peace. The scripture tells us how to overcome him:

> "And they overcame him by the blood of the Lamb, and by the word of their testimony..."
> Revelation 12:11

Knowing Christ as our Savior and speaking out the goodness of God, what He has done for us, covers us with the blood of Jesus and overcomes the enemy. As we decide not to accept the accusations and lies, replacing the devil's lies with truth from God's word, our soul is set free from guilt. Choosing what to think and what to speak is a battle that requires discipline and courage. Not everyone is going to agree with us when we choose truth. Though backlash can be cruel, we hold fast to the faith that we have; it increases with each step. Grace gives us strength to win the war.

Chapter 10

Grace Wins

It was June 29, 1997, Sunday morning, what would have been Andy's eighteenth birthday. I awoke early and went to the living room to pray. There alone, I accepted the fact that this would be a painful day. I sat, expecting sorrow and grief to flood into my heart and mind. When it did not, I got up and began to get ready for church, sure that the sorrow would come eventually.

Was I ever wrong! That is not how God wants us to live. We think circumstances and emotions should rule our lives when God gave us all power in Christ Jesus to rule over emotions and circumstances.

Suddenly, I became aware of an increasing joy rising inside of me for no apparent reason. I spoke the words quietly in surprise, "I'm being filled with the Holy Spirit." Only God could have revealed that, since I could not remember anything like this ever happening. As the joy became greater, excitement joined it. This was not something I had conjured up on my own; I was expecting grief and sorrow.

I came out of my bedroom and started down the hall. Donald was sitting in a chair in the living room. He had been called the night before, at the last minute, by our music director to sing in church this morning. She did not know today was Andy's birthday, nor did she know that the Lord had given Donald an arrangement of "It is Well with My Soul" to sing days earlier.

Donald had not known when he would sing it, but God did. When he spoke to the music director by phone, Saturday night, Donald told her he was not surprised she'd called and already had the song he would sing. God's timing was perfect. As I walked by his chair, I laid my hand on his shoulder and said, "You are going to be a witness to many people today." I had no idea of the full impact of that statement, but I had been filled with the Holy Spirit and everything was exciting!

By the time I got to Sunday School, my body could hardly contain the overwhelming joy that had filled me. I wanted to jump up and down, shout, do anything but sit still. The teacher did not know what to do with me as she taught, trying to ignore my barely restrained jubilation. I tried to sit and listen.

Her subject included the very same thoughts I had been having that week—how the Holy Spirit was bringing us, as believers, into like-mindedness and how what was being revealed to one was being revealed to others, so that when we came back together, we had the same teaching. It was exciting to see the Spirit moving among His people and bringing unity.

I made it through Sunday School—exuberantly, I might add—but the church worship service proved even more difficult to endure. By that time, trying to stay in my seat was a battle. My body was moving involuntarily all over! I wrapped my arms around my waist and gripped the back of the chair with both hands trying to just stay seated. My sister, not knowing the Holy Spirit had taken over my emotions, leaned over to me and said, "For someone who does not like to have attention drawn to her, you are really making a scene." Later, she told me my feet were moving constantly. I had no idea; I was just trying to stay in the chair.

The pastor said something about the early service congregation being asleep. I leaned over to my friend on the other side of me and, trying to contain some of my excitement, stated, "It won't be like that in this service!" She looked at me cautiously and smiled politely. She probably thought I had lost my mind.

As the service started, hymns were sung and announcements were made. I could have easily been miserable trying to hold myself still, except that I had so much joy...joy unspeakable, from an unseen Source:

> "Whom having not seen, ye love; in whom, though now ye see Him not, yet believing, ye rejoice with joy unspeakable and full of glory:" 1 Peter 1:8

I looked back at Donald working the sound mixer for the service and prayed for him. Matt, who was sitting with his dad, later told me that he had seen Donald's hands shaking and had prayed for him also.

When Donald stepped in front of the microphone to speak, I knew the Lord was with him. Through his slightly nervous and broken voice, he gave his testimony of the past year. The Lord directed his words, even adding a bit of humor (God loves humor; He invented it). Donald had struggled with Andy's death and had even been angry with God at first. He talked about how all was not well with his soul last year, but now it was, praise God! He began to sing. Donald sang with such strength and power, everyone knew it was God revealing His faithfulness through the words and the man. What a service! Almost every hand was raised in praise to God all over that Baptist sanctuary. The Holy Spirit was once again moving among His people as we gave praise to the One who gives us peace.

As tears streamed down my face, I praised God and thanked Him for what He had done in Donald's life. I also knew that if I allowed one part of my body to become unrestrained I would no longer be in my chair, but only God knows where. I would be an embarrassment to my sister, my friend next to me, and Donald, not to mention my teenage son. God only knows what the people in my church would say! So, I held on physically, my hands gripping the back of the chair, while my spirit leapt and danced for joy within me, trying to take my body with it.

After the service, the exceedingly great joy that had overwhelmed me through most of the service had somewhat subsided. People came to Donald and me to tell us how they were touched by his singing and how he was anointed by the Holy Spirit. We were aware of God's hand on Donald and were so grateful for His presence. For the rest of the day, our family was on the mountaintop, thanking God for all He had done.

On what could have been a day of painful memories, the Lord made a day of true joy and praise. I wondered why God had filled me with His Spirit. I was not ministering to anyone; in fact, it was almost unbearable to contain such joy.

All I know is that God chose His way to erase any sorrow or grief, to help me be an encouragement to Donald, and to cause me to offer continual praises to Him for His goodness. He shows up in mysterious ways!

The amazing grace of God's goodness brings light to the darkness. Hagar and her son were cast out of the only home she knew, sent into the wilderness with only bread and a container of water. When the water ran out and there was none around, she placed her son under a bush and went a distance from him because she did not want to watch him die. There alone in the wilderness, Hagar saw no hope. She was ready for the worst: her own death and the death of her son, and she did not want to see it. Hagar's son was not the son of Abraham's promise from God. She and her son had both been rejected, and rightly so. Why should anyone care for them?

God cared. He called to Hagar and asked what was wrong. He had heard the cries of her son. God cares about what we care about. His heart is touched by what touches our hearts. God told her to lift up the boy; He would make her son a great nation. God opened Hagar's eyes to see a well of water, just what she needed to save the boy's life, but there was more—a promise. Ishmael would not only live, but he would thrive. A great nation would come from him. That day, God's grace poured out upon a woman who had no husband and her child had been kicked out of his father's house. Grace brought hope for a great future in what looked like the darkest time of Hagar's life.

Through God's grace, there is a plan for us, much greater than the enemy's attacks. When darkness plans an assault, Grace plans a victory.

The assault the enemy had planned on Andy's birthday was overcome with God's great weapon of joy. The joy of the Lord had been our strength. The enemy could not assault us with grief because the Lord poured out His great joy.

63

Chapter 11

Supernatural Grace

In January 1998, a friend of mine who had been a support to me through the time following Andy's death asked me to a Bible study she was attending. I had been very leery of the things that went on in this Bible study in the past and tried to warn my friend about them, yet I could not deny the change I had seen in her. She was sweeter, and her knowledge of God had increased. I wanted to learn what she had learned, so I went.

I attended the Bible study prepared to test the spirits:

> "Beloved, believe not every spirit, but try the spirits whether they are of God: because many false prophets are gone out into the world." John 4:1

I could hardly believe it when the person leading the Bible study started off by teaching on how to test the spirits and not to believe everyone who came to us. I thanked God; He knew my heart. I stayed in the back, watching. My friend had invited me even though she knew how I felt about the manifestation of the gifts of the Holy Spirit—unfavorably. I just watched and asked for God's discernment, still being unsure and not too certain this was right for me. I was glad when I had to leave early to pick Matt up from school.

The following morning, while in prayer, I asked God if the study group was of Him: the speaking in tongues, prophecy, and being "slain in the spirit." I made a list of pros and cons. The pros were:

1. Jesus was glorified through the teaching of the word of God and in thanking Him for all that took place at the meeting. The Bible teaching had been in-depth and filled with scripture. I knew truth must be backed up with God's word, and it was.

2. My own private prayer time changed the very next day. I offered more praise to God, which is what was done at the meeting. Without realizing it, I spent more time in prayer. The time went by so quickly.

3. Love was abundant at the meeting.

4. Scripture was brought to life for me. It became more personal and meaningful.

There were really no cons, except that I was about to find out what it meant to be verbally persecuted for attending.

I missed the next study, which was a relief, because it was a lot to handle. I went to the April meeting two months later, on my forty-first birthday. A gentle rebuking from the Lord came from a very sweet woman I did not know. It was about marriage and it was painfully true. It spoke of how we need to lift our husbands up, stop beating them down, and to be a help to them. The message seemed to go on and on. A prophecy was spoken over me for ministry. This was all very new to me. At home, I began praying more fervently for my marriage and for specific areas that were pointed out in the meeting. God began changing me. I could feel more compassion growing in me for Donald.

I asked God more questions about this group. One question was, "Why does God seem to manifest Himself here and not in other places?" Shortly after I began seeking an answer to this, a man in our church, unknowingly, answered the question while filling in for our pastor. He preached from an Old Testament verse:

> "It came even to pass, as the trumpeters and singers were as one, to make one sound to be heard in praising and thanking the LORD; and when they lifted up their voice with the trumpets and cymbals and instruments of music, and praised the LORD, saying, For the Lord is good; for His mercy endureth for ever: that then the house was filled with a cloud, even the house of the LORD; So that the priests could not stand to minister by reason of the cloud: for the glory of the LORD had filled the house of God." 2 Chronicles 5:13–14

That scripture hit me like a ton of bricks. "That's it," I thought. We always began with scripture and songs praising God. God inhabits the praises of His people. That is why we saw such glory. It was true worship in spirit and in truth, not just singing songs. Hearts were unified in seeking God's presence. I thanked God for understanding.

Other questions about the Bible study group were answered by the pastor and teachers at my own church as they ministered. It seemed my church and the Bible study group were crossing over into each other's subject matter without either assembly knowing it. The people at our church would not believe in the things that were happening in the Bible study meetings I was attending, but God was using their own mouths with His words to confirm for me the truths of it. How many times has God given us His truth right before our eyes but we would not believe?

As I continued to attend monthly meetings, more and more scripture was made alive to me. God was opening understanding of the supernatural life He had given to us in Him. What opened my eyes to see that God has a path for our life that leads to joy, was the scripture stating:

> "Thou wilt show me the path of life: in thy pres-
> ence is fullness of joy; at thy right hand there
> are pleasures forevermore." Psalms 16:11

God was revealing the path of life. It included praise and spending more time with Him. Following His path led to joy and peace in His presence. That path corrected and instructed our lives, bringing us deeper and deeper into His truth.

The scripture also revealed how much He cared for me and the things I cared about:

> "The Lord will perfect that which concerneth
> me..." Psalms 138:8

God was bringing all the things for which I had been praying into right order. I could leave them in His hands and not worry, which was exactly what He wanted me to do.

The Bible study group joined together to pray for our husbands and fast one meal a day for a month. God began giving me scripture to speak out loud to Donald, making it personal, such as:

> "Blessed is the man that walketh not in the counsel of the ungodly, nor standeth in the way of sinners, nor sitteth in the seat of the scornful. But his delight is in the law of the LORD; and in his law doth he meditate day and night. And he shall be like a tree planted by the rivers of water, that bringeth forth his fruit in his season; his leaf also shall not wither; and whatsoever he doeth shall prosper." Psalm 1:1–3

I began calling him a godly man and a mighty man of valor from Judges 6:12, and more as the situation called for it. I was not really seeing it, but God was. When I spoke out these scriptural words of encouragement to him, Donald looked at me like I had lost my mind, but later he told me they had encouraged him. What was surprising was the change in me. God was teaching me many things in a short amount of time. The manifestation of the gifts, something I had shunned for many years, was now opening greater revelation of God to me. This is just what I had been praying for God to show me, before I had attended this group.

God spoke to me: *"No one man and no one religion has it all. When you put them all together, like a big jigsaw puzzle, you will see a bigger picture of Me.*" He also told me, "*You* (I knew He meant "you and your denomination") *have had a form of godliness but denied my power.*" I understood that to deny the Holy Spirit's supernatural power was a serious offense against God.

Months later, I was at a meeting where a woman who did not know me prophesied that God had heard my prayers about wanting a new house without debt, and that I would be speaking in front of many people. She could not know that I had written in my prayer book that week, very timidly, asking God for a new house without debt, and that just a few days earlier, I had been asked to speak for a group of women from several churches in Waycross, Georgia. This prophecy gift scared me. In fact, two of my good friends who had come with me flew the coop and left me behind alone in the meeting. It was too weird for them, but I was too hungry for God not to stay and find out the truth. I only knew of ungodly psychics doing this sort of thing, and I asked God to show me in His word if this was of Him. I knew He would protect me if I was seeking for Him and not just for selfish motives. Later, at home, the Holy Spirit led me to scripture, where Paul taught how prophesy revealed the secrets of the heart and caused man to worship God:

> "But if all prophesy, and there come in one that believeth not, or one unlearned, he is convinced of all, he is judged of all: And thus, are the secrets of his heart made manifest; and so falling down on his face he will worship God, and report that God is in you of a truth." 1 Corinthians 14:24–25

God's supernatural grace gave spiritual gifts to men, and to deny them was to deny His power:

> "Having a form of godliness but denying the power thereof: from such turn away." 2 Timothy 3:5

We can be Christians and only be experiencing a small portion of the life God gave us to enjoy. He has so much more for us than we are willing to accept. It comes with a price and a battle. The closer we get to God and the more we accept His way of revealing Himself, the stronger we become. Satan hates for us to grow, but God loves it. The devil will send people to criticize us and cause fear, as he did with my two friends who deserted me. We are to believe:

> "And these signs shall follow them that believe; In my name shall they cast out devils; they shall speak with new tongues; They shall take up serpents; and if they drink any deadly thing, it shall not hurt them; they shall lay hands on the sick, and they shall recover." Mark 16:17–18

The gifts work by faith. Faith works by love. The more we walk in the spirit, the more we will love Him and His people.

The Bible study group, which I had been afraid to attend and then was criticized for attending—by my own church members—helped open my eyes to God's power. God's supernatural gifts are for our strengthening and encouragement against a supernatural enemy that hates us. Even Donald's faith was increased. He had a touch from God that totally changed his life and set him free. We both were strengthened through hard times and were given hope to move on from our pain into joy. I no longer denied God's power but submitted to Him.

I asked God if I should continue in this prayer group. Just before the October 1998 meeting, the Lord spoke to me and said, "*You have learned all you can here.*" I thought that, surely, I must be misunderstanding the message. I knew so little, but when I told it to my sister who had been attending with me, she said she had received the same message and had also doubted if she had understood it correctly. We went to one more meeting, then the group ended suddenly. I continued with a smaller group, still seeking God's direction with every step. Donald was now hearing God's voice. The Lord spoke to him and said, "*Support her in this.*" I drew strength from these ladies as God broke down religious barriers that prevented truth from being known.

In a Wednesday night prayer meeting at our church, one of the leaders stood up and began to speak: "There are women going to prayer groups, and the things that are happening there are causing the church to laugh and jeer at them."

"Laugh and jeer" at other church members? That is supposed to be good church behavior? There were more derogatory remarks made, and then he prayed for God to help those people get out of the groups. My sister excitedly asked me later, "Are we being persecuted?" I nodded somberly. She was thrilled...me, not so much. I knew what the Bible said about rejoicing when men revile you, but it still was not fun.

"Blessed are they which are persecuted for righteousness' sake: for theirs is the kingdom of heaven." Revelation 12:11

There is liberty in Christ. He will do what He pleases when He pleases for anyone who will believe Him. God hates denominational and racial barriers. He wants them broken down within the church body. When God shows up in a group, no one cares where you go to church, what you believe, or what background influenced you. Jesus becomes the focus, and His Spirit unites us all. I love crossing over man's religious barriers. Breaking the barriers brings liberty, and with Christ there is liberty and freedom.

Each person must work out his own salvation with a holy reverence, praying that God will help us not to think we are above being taught. He is wonderful at abasing the proud. We are to be clothed with humility and meekness, knowing that He is faithful, which is often difficult to accept. The fear of man cannot be our guide. I always wanted to do what was right, follow the rules. I was learning that the rules that exist in serving God are His, not man's, and sometimes they may seem a little unruly.

My faith was growing. I felt like God was changing my world at rocket speed and it was exciting, albeit a little scary, but I loved the adventure.

Chapter 12

Grace for New Levels

A couple of ladies were making an album in Donald's recording studio behind our house and had stepped outside for a break. I came out of the house at the same time and we began talking. Still being full of excitement about all God had done for us, I briefly shared with them some highlights of His miraculous goodness regarding Andy. They wanted to hear more. I was happy to continue with the details.

When I finished, they both wanted me to present this wonderful testimony to their church. I was terrified of public speaking, so there was no way I was going to stand in front of an entire church and pour out my heart. I let them know I had no desire to speak in public, yet they were persistent, even in their departure saying that they would have their church leader call me.

Later, while I was alone, thinking it was over, God spoke His mind to me. *"When you are asked to speak, do it."* His voice was now my life's essential element for survival, and His instruction was my command. The choice was clear: I had to do it. Like Christ, I was compelled to live by every word of His mouth. I knew that nothing else could work in this life.

> "Jesus saith unto them, My meat is to do the
> will of Him that sent me, and to finish His
> work." John 4:34

Just a few days later, while taking out a load of clothes to wash, all my joints suddenly became weak and wobbly like Jell-O. Dull pain ran up my legs. Having been a nurse in the ICU, I immediately began diagnosing myself with all kinds of terminal illnesses. I tried to figure out how I could contact Donald, so he could take me to the hospital. He was only a few feet away in the recording studio, but within seconds, I was so weak and in so much pain that all I could do was cling to the dryer for support. Suddenly, the Holy Spirit spoke to me: "*This is the enemy.*" He was urging me to rebuke Satan.

I was trying to hold my body upright by leaning on the dryer, where I had struggled to get while carrying the load of clothes. I was not comfortable with rebuking Satan, so in an effort to maintain some dignity and self-respect, despite all my pain and suffering, I looked out the door to make sure no one was around to hear me before I said out loud, "Satan, I rebuke you in the name of Jesus. I am going to speak in Waycross, no matter what!" Immediately, my joints strengthened and the pain disappeared. I praised God for His wisdom and power. I had learned in the Bible study group that I had power over all the power of the enemy:

> "Behold, I give unto you power to tread on ser-
> pents and scorpions, and over all the power

of the enemy: and nothing shall by any means
hurt you." Luke 10:19

When the church leader from Waycross called, I emphatically stated, "Yes, I will speak. No matter what happens, even if I'm in traction, I will be there!"

Five days after the bold acceptance for my first real speaking engagement, the bottom seemed to fall out of my life with some very personal devastating news concerning a family member. I was sure, with this new development, that everything had changed; I would have to cancel. However, God, in all His greatness, prevails over bad news. He reminded me of my position in Him through scripture:

"He shall not be afraid of evil tidings: his heart
is fixed, trusting in the LORD." Psalms 112:7

God spoke to me concerning the "evil tidings" I had received: *This is not a mountain, only a bump in the road to get everyone back on track.*" That put things in perspective; where I had seen a mountain, God saw a bump in the road.

Satan gave it his best shot to try and stop me from speaking, but the scriptures I had learned and the revealing of the "exceeding greatness of His power" in me gave me strength to keep fighting.

"...the exceeding greatness of his power
to us-ward who believe, according to the
working of his mighty power." Ephesians 1:19

We make more out of things than they are just because human nature says we should fall apart or break down. God expects us to stand strong, take authority, and overcome.

It is common knowledge to God and all of Heaven that we are fighting an unseen enemy. It does not seem to be common knowledge to God's people.

I accepted the engagement five weeks prior to the event. During those five weeks, there were more attacks that were vicious and continuous. Satan relentlessly bombarded me during those weeks. One type of attack was the words he spoke to my mind, "Who are you to tell others about God? You've failed miserably in your life."

I asked God, "Knowing me, how can I speak to all those ladies?"

His Holy Spirit spoke quietly, "*You are not telling them about you; you are telling them about me.*" I smiled as instant peace relieved my fears. I thanked Him, again.

I thought that if those five weeks would not hurry and pass, we might lose everything the way Satan was viciously attacking our home, health, finances, and relationships, but God is so faithful!

During one of my prayer times in my bedroom, with my face to the floor asking God for the strength to speak in front of people, God gave me a vision. He showed me that I was taking a large step of faith by accepting this speaking engagement. I saw myself stepping easily over a very deep gorge, smiling, giving no attention to the danger. His word, the sword of the Spirit, was in my right hand, meaning I had His word in my heart.

As I came out of the prayer and vision, it seemed as if I had been in another place. I thought I had prayed only a few minutes, but when I looked at the clock, it had been about an hour. When I tried to get off the floor, I was surprised at how weak I was. I had to get ready to go out with friends and I could hardly get myself dressed. With each passing moment, I pushed myself to get ready. Strength slowly returned, along with joy, and my energy increased. I knew that I had been in the presence of the Lord during my prayer. He had been strengthening my spirit to do His will. The remainder of the day I was almost childlike. It seemed all my fears and cares were gone. They had been replaced with joy and lightheartedness. The peace was unexplainable. Grace that was more than sufficient was abundant for this speaking engagement.

On November 9, 1998, I stepped up to the platform to speak in Waycross. Draped from the walls of the church were beautiful, airy billows of snow-white, chiffon-like fabric. Pure white cloths covered the rows of tables, which displayed intricately carved ceramic doves resting in the center of each. It looked like Heaven. It was the perfect setting for my testimony.

I was led and seated to what was the VIP table, which was even more elaborately decorated. I had never been treated with such honor. Tricia and two of my friends who had wanted to come were seated with me.

The room was filled with women who seemed full of nonjudgmental, curious anticipation of what would come from me, the visiting speaker. Instead of one church, there were five churches of women represented and waiting patiently. They had been told nothing of my testimony.

Immediately, fear hit me. I had always avoided being in front of people, yet somehow now I was the guest of honor. I was the speaker. What God had done for me was the reason the room was decorated so beautifully.

After the first few words of speaking, the Holy Spirit took over like I had never imagined or could have planned. Shirley, who had wanted to go with me, told me she knew the precise moment the Holy Spirit "clicked in." Fear left, and I began to speak freely. As I listened to my own voice, it sounded too sweet to be mine. It crossed my mind, "I must be making Tricia [my sister sitting in the front row] sick. She knows I don't talk this sweetly."

The words flowed with ease and grace. No one moved. It seemed so important to tell what God had done for me so that these ladies would know He could do it for them. This message of hope was finally being told and defeating the enemy. All of Satan's tactics to try and stop this time from coming had failed. His plans had been canceled. We overcome him by the blood of the Lamb and the word of our testimony. It was no wonder that he'd wanted to close my mouth.

I spoke for what I thought was ten minutes, when I heard the Holy Spirit say, "*Stop.*" "Well, that's not much to say, but I have to stop," I thought. The videotape Donald had recorded showed that I had spoken twenty-nine minutes. Exiting the platform, I heard all the chairs being pushed back as the people were getting up. I thought, "They sure are anxious to leave." Suddenly, I heard clapping. Women all over the room were giving a standing ovation. I sat in my chair, head down, and prayed, "God, make them stop. I can't take this!"

He spoke back to me, "*It's not for you; it's for Me.*" I laughed. Again, it was not about me. I joined in with them. From all that God was teaching me, accepting the speaking engagement, and through the battles that had been won, I had gone to another level of spiritual growth. I have heard it said, "New levels, new devils." There sure were. It seemed with every step of grace there were more attacks . Thank

God that as spiritual growth was being worked out, I was also growing in grace.

Chapter 13

Sacrificial Grace

I had given up my full time ICU position as a nurse to be home more with the boys and began working at a branch of the local high school as a school nurse and teacher about a year before Andy went home to be with the Lord. I kept a part-time position in the ICU, allowing me the choice to work as I was available. For the last few months of his life, I was working more hours to make extra money because Andy had been chosen for the opportunity to go to Boston with a few select students whose interests were in the medical field. He would need a suit for each day, plane tickets, and lodging. He never made it to Boston, however, and God had different directions in mind for the rest of our family, as well as for my career.

Weeks after Andy's death, the Lord revealed to me that I was to homeschool Matt. He actually spoke three commands to me as he told me: *"You have raised your children the world's way, now do it mine—no dating, no church youth groups, and homeschool. There is no difference between the church youth and the world."*

Matt and a girl at church had been sitting together. He was not old enough to date, so that was not a problem with the instructions of no dating. Homeschooling seemed unnecessary because I was working in the school Matt would attend the next year. I would be close to him. It did not make sense to take him out. Also, I was the youth leader of the church youth group he would attend, so what was the problem with that?

This was so foreign to me. There were families that homeschooled their children in our church, and frankly, I tried to stay away from them.

God had said no dating. One of my first thoughts was, "How will Matt ever meet a girl and get married? Is he going to live with us forever?" I felt like I would be cutting out everything in his life but breathing.

Teaching in the public-school system, I knew this was not going to go over very well with the system-dependent faculty. As the youth leader, I would have to explain this to our church, where some already thought I was from another planet. With Matt and the girl at church, I knew that relationship would not last long; they were nothing alike. These new instructions from God were going to change our lives dramatically.

It was God's voice, so each step had to be taken. There was no choice as to whether to obey or not. God does not suggest, He commands lovingly for our own good, and His voice was paramount in my life. I moved cautiously with His wisdom. I waited patiently for the girlfriend/boyfriend relationship to end, which it did within a few days. By me not saying anything to Matt, only watching and waiting, I kept down any unnecessary rebellion. That only left two more commands to approach delicately with Donald and Matt, removing Matt from the church youth group and beginning home school.

Matt, going into the eighth grade, thought homeschooling was a great idea; Donald was not quite as excited. He did not want Matt to be homeschooled, so I waited. Yes, I knew that I had heard from God and that was top priority, but I also knew that we had to be in agreement for this to work. I prayed, "God, I will not fight with Donald on this. I do not believe that is what You want. We have had enough drama. You will have to change his heart and mind." He did.

Following a Sunday worship service, Donald was standing outside the church with me and a friend, listening to her tell about her elementary-age daughter's dilemmas in the public school. She came to a story of painful attacks on her daughter by other students that brought tears to my eyes. Suddenly, Donald was sold. Soon after, I heard him tell someone, "We are homeschooling Matt." That is how I found out Donald had changed his mind about homeschooling. How easy it was to let God take care of it.

I kept Matt in school for the next year. He was entering the eighth grade and I continued working to keep things as normal as possible that first year following Andy's death. It would give us time to adjust emotionally without any other big changes to handle. God gave wisdom, discernment, and understanding to move with precision into His will for our family at the right time. He had a strategy for His plan to take shape. Grace was working.

God took care of every detail. I knew the people with whom I worked at the high school would not be too fond of this new development. I entered my office one morning for work to find two of the staff from guidance and one office worker. The guidance counselor had everything but a power point presentation detailing all the reasons I could not homeschool. I had hoped to keep the decision a secret to avoid such confrontations, but it had somehow gotten out. I listened patiently to every word, then stated, "This is not my decision. It's God's." I smiled. For some reason, I thought that would settle it, but he did not look convinced as he threw a stack of school requirements for education on my desk, and demanded, "Can you do all this?" He exited my office in a huff.

Matt was a good musician. Even at thirteen years old, he excelled in playing the saxophone in the middle-school band. I answered the phone one morning in my office/clinic to hear the high school bandleader on the other end fuming.

"I hear you are going to homeschool Matt."

"Yes," I answered.

Almost yelling, he continued, "You know he will not be able to play in the high school band. Homeschoolers can't take extracurricular classes."

I calmly replied, "This is not my decision, it's God's. He is the One that gave Matt his talent, He will open the doors for him." The bandleader acknowledged what I said and hung up. I had peace. I knew the band director wanted Matt in the high school band and was frustrated that it looked like he was not going to be able to play. Grace had covered me for all these confrontations and for the ones that would come from more people who did not understand.

In a few months, the band director called back; I could hear the joy in his voice. "There has been legislature passed in Florida that says homeschoolers can take extracurricular classes."

I laughed. "God is so good! He knows what He's doing."

I felt a little awkward, but after researching, talking to those other homeschooling parents whom I had tried to avoid, and going to seminars, we began homeschooling with Matt's ninth-grade year. We got in the groove as I quit my full-time job at the high school and signed Matt up with the county office as a homeschooled student.

Early one morning while I was watching a Bible teacher on TV, the Lord showed me another change in my life that had to be made. The teacher stated that many times we hold on to things that God is finished with in our lives, like trying to ride a dead horse. Until we let go of those, we cannot reach the higher things God has for us. I had lived with some oppression on me for nine years. Many times, I felt like I could hardly put one foot in front of the other. As I listened to this Bible teacher, the Holy Spirit spoke to me, *"The oppression is coming from nursing."* I thought, "From nursing?" I could not let go of my license. I had worked so hard for it! I knew the Lord had wanted me to quit my job with the school system, even though I loved working with the kids, so I could homeschool Matt. Making this tough decision brought priceless blessings, such as drawing our family closer and releasing Matt from so much of the peer pressure that had tormented Andy. Homeschooling also allowed for God to be brought into the teachings that were not taught in public school. Now, the Lord was revealing to me that I was to quit my part-time job working in the ICU in a local hospital. This was difficult to do because I could work when I wanted. It kept up some very important nursing skills that I knew I would lose if I did not use them regularly, but despite my concern, for the sake of obedience, I quit. I had peace in letting go of such a stressful job; still, I was sure I would keep my RN license current for future use. Who knew what might happen that may require me to go back to work?

I sat arguing with God, "Surely, you know that people will think I am really crazy for putting so much time and effort into schooling just to let it all go and have no job security." The Lord was not concerned about what people would think. He was not concerned about me securing my own financial future. He was wanting me to lean totally on Him, to let go of everything that made me think I was in control. Finally, I said, "Lord, I release my license to you." With that statement, I felt a gentle physical drawing or pulling of my head and shoulders, then the oppression was gone. Just then, on the TV, a man and woman began singing a praise song called "Free at Last." How appropriate. I was now free at last.

That morning, I had planned to go to an all-day class to obtain credits to keep my license, but instead I joined with the ladies of my Sunday School class in prayer and Bible study and had a great time.

> "Yea doubtless, and I count all things but loss
> for the excellency of the knowledge of Christ
> Jesus my Lord: for whom I have suffered the
> loss of all things, and do count them but dung,
> that I may win Christ." Philippians 3:8

Giving up what we have worked so hard to obtain is difficult, but there are seasons in our lives, and all things are not for all time. Recognizing that God is doing something new or different is uncomfortable to say the least, but He gives us grace to sacrifice what seems so important to us.

Sometimes we hold positions, careers, reputations, people, etc. tighter than we hold on to Him.

In Genesis 22, Abraham was told to take his son, the son all his promises rested in, and sacrifice him on an altar to God. The Bible shows no hesitation on Abraham's part to be obedient. It does not show Abraham telling Sarah what he is going to do, a smart move on his part.

Abraham told the young men he'd brought with him to stay back while he and Isaac went on to worship. Abraham assured the young men they would be back. The New Testament, Hebrews 11:19, reveals that Abraham already believed Isaac would be raised from the dead because he trusted God to fulfill the promises. While Abraham was sure he would have to perform the horrible act of killing his son, he trusted God to work it out. The sacrifice was planned, and Abraham was willing. We know the Lord stopped Abraham short of putting a knife to his son's throat. God now knew that Abraham loved Him and trusted Him even over his own son. He passed the test, and the abundant blessings would flow from generation to generation.

God loves our children more than we do, and the only way He can bless them is if we release them into His hands. If God could release His own precious Son into the hands of the enemy, surely, we can release our children into His hands. He gives grace to those who do.

Chapter 14

Grace Marie

Approximately four weeks following Andy's death, I was at a ladies' retreat with our church for a couple days, at the insistence of my husband and son. The first evening, the ladies and I were sitting around talking before going to bed when the Holy Spirit spoke to me in a prophetic manner. One lady was telling of a miraculous healing regarding a family member whose name was Grace. As soon as she stated the woman's name, Grace, I heard a voice in my spirit that said, *"That will be the name of your next child, Grace."*

Silently, I immediately responded, "I'm not having any more children." Silence. I was thirty-nine years old and I was not interested in having another baby.

I did not share this with anyone for about three weeks. While talking to Denise on the phone one morning, I silently asked God if I should tell her this new revelation. I heard a baby cry in the background. Denise stated she had company with a baby girl at her house. Since Denise seldom had babies at her house and the baby was a girl, I took this as a possible sign that I should tell her about Grace. What could it hurt?

Denise responded to my news without much enthusiasm, and I regretted telling her. Me having a baby seemed ridiculous. When the phone rang the next morning, I picked it up to hear Denise bursting with excitement as she spoke, "Dawn! Are you sitting down?"

"Yes," I said, laughing because of her enthusiasm.

"Dawn," she said, "you are going to have a baby!"

Laughing again, I said, "No, I'm not."

Vibrantly, Denise kept talking. "I had a dream last night. No people were in it, only voices, mine and God's. God said you are going to have a baby. I told God that He could not replace Andy. I can't believe I was arguing with God! Then, God told me He was not replacing Andy; He was blessing you." She had two more dreams concerning Grace, seeing her and talking to her in the dreams. I was amazed at the dreams and thought about them for days, but I did not feel comfortable telling Donald.

About two months later, Donald and I were sitting on the sofa in the living room. Suddenly, he closed his eyes and shook his head violently, as if he were trying to get something out of his mind. "What's wrong?" I asked.

"Nothing," Donald responded almost harshly. For about ten minutes I gently coaxed him to tell me what he was thinking. I knew it had to be something from God. Finally, he told me. Starting about a week after Andy's death, something had been telling him about a plate. It was one out of a set of decorative, painted plates hanging on the wall in the dining room. This certain plate portrayed a pretty little girl. The "something" told Donald that she was his daughter. Excitedly, I told him for the first time about the words I had heard regarding Grace and Denise's dreams. He was very quiet, and we did not talk about it much.

As the days went by, I was trying to think of a middle name to go with Grace. While driving in the car one day, the name Marie came to me. I liked it and kept it to myself.

A few nights later, while I was sitting in the den, Donald walked in and said, "I think I've thought of a middle name to go with Grace." He continued, "Marie." I could hardly believe it, and neither could he when I told him the exact same thought had come to me. The Holy Spirit had unified our thoughts, and it was more confirmation of Grace's coming. Donald walked out of the den, not wanting to talk about it anymore. He was not yet comfortable with this supernatural revealing of thoughts and hearing God speak. I patiently waited for him to be the one to bring it up again.

Our faith increased as we dared to talk about Grace Marie openly. We did not hear from God regarding her until about two years later, when He spoke to Donald. The Holy Spirit spoke clearly, "*When it is time, go into your wife and I will give you a daughter. Her name will be called Grace and she will bring my love and mercy into your home.*" It was exciting to hear from God again, but we were still uncertain as to what "when it is time" was referring. The clock was ticking, and at the time of this writing, we still wait to see how God is going to work this out.

The Bible gives instruction for receiving vision for the future from God. For God's children, it should not be uncommon for us to hear God speak and give His upcoming plans. That is why the instruction is given in His word:

> "And the LORD answered me, and said, 'Write
> the vision, and make it plain upon tables, that

he may run that readeth it. For the vision is yet for an appointed time, but at the end it shall speak, and not lie: though it tarry, wait for it; because it will surely come, it will not tarry.'" Habakkuk 2:2–3.

When God gives us a vision for the future, He wants us to write it down. The promise gives us hope and a future to look forward to seeing come to pass. We can easily forget the promise as life begins to look like it is going in another direction, but if we truly believe God is not a man and He cannot lie, we can stand on that written promise. When we read it out loud, it gets deep down in our soul to renew our hope and vision. God's written word is truth. God's word spoken deep in our spirit is truth. God's vision to us is truth. Every lie from the devil, the world, and our own flesh is defeated when truth is proclaimed. If we want to see the vision come to pass, sometimes we must be the only one believing it and speaking it. We may have to write it and post it up on our mirror in the bathroom so that every day we will be reminded of the truth God has given us.

Abram had a promise from God: a great, vast amount of land for him and his descendants. Following that promise, Abram had to leave his family, fight in a war, and refuse the temptation of a big payoff from a heathen king. With all this testing, God was watching.

Abram proved to be a man who could not be bought. God was looking for a few good men and Abram measured up; the promise of blessings began to flow. God spoke to him:

"Do not fear, Abram. I am your shield, your protection from your enemies. I am your exceeding great reward. I will be the One that blesses you far above and beyond anyone else." Genesis 15:11 (my paraphrase)

There was something Abram had his heart set on, a child. Nothing was greater than having children to bless and carry on the lineage of a family. Abram boldly approached God, basically saying:

> "If you are my exceeding great reward, then what are you going to do about me being childless? What about the greatest reward you can give me, a child? Right now, my servant is my heir because you have not given me any children." Genesis 15:2–3 (my paraphrase)

God's heart was in the cry of Abram. God wanted to create a nation from the seed of Abram. God was delighted Abram asked for a child and responded:

> "Your servant will not be your heir, but one that is born of your own seed. Look at the stars, your descendants will be as many as the stars which cannot be numbered." Genesis 15:4–5 (my paraphrase)

God counted Abram righteous because he believed God. Abram, being a man, needed to see the promise in his heart. To get it embedded, God gave His plan for that, too. An animal sacrifice, requiring blood, would seal the covenant. Abram waited for God to show up and receive the offering of the animals he had killed. Birds and vultures tried to steal his covenant promise sacrifice. He had to keep them shooed off.

When we are waiting for the promise, we must keep the doubt, unbelief, and lies shooed off from our sacrifice of obedience and waiting period so that we do not lose confidence in God's word to us. There is an appointed time for the vision to come into reality. It will not tarry beyond the appointed time. Waiting for it and reading it out loud keeps faith alive in us. There may be others who can believe and help carry the promise. One thing is certain: if God spoke it and we believe it, it will come.

God showed up for Abram with a great miraculous encounter that provided him a look at the future hundreds of years ahead. Abram saw the future for his descendants, it was embedded in his soul. He could not erase it. It was too great. His faithfulness in believing and waiting was bringing God's promises to pass.

Years later, God confirmed the promise again. Abram needed a Post-it note on his mirror, so to speak, to keep him reminded of the promise. God told Abram, "I will bring about the promise of our covenant. I have made you a father of many nations. Your new name is Abraham." "Abraham" meant "father of many nations." Even though it did not look that way, every time Abraham was called by his new name, the prophetic promise was proclaimed and declared, "Hey, Father of Many Nations." Abraham would be reminded that he was the father of descendants as numerous as the stars. The lies would be dispelled with truth.

The scripture reveals how important it is to decree and declare:

"Thou shalt also decree a thing, and it shall
be established unto thee: and the light shall
shine upon thy ways." Job 22:28

"I will declare the decree: the LORD hath said
unto me..." Psalms 2:7

When we decree a thing that God has shown us, it is established to us. It has become ours because we have received it. More light, insight, understanding shines on our way. When we declare the decree, the vision God has given us, we embed it into our soul, keeping it alive. It will surely come. God gives us grace to believe, to wait, and to keep the vision alive.

Teachings from Time with God

As I was spending time with the Lord in the years following Andy's death, a picture of a legal-size writing pad kept coming into my mind. I knew I had to purchase one and begin to write what God was teaching me. I never imagined those notes would become sermons. Out of this testimony, a church was birthed, Grace Harbor. The Lord Jesus has been that safe harbor of grace for my family and me. Following are some of those messages.

Chapter 15

Rebuilding the Walls

The precious walls of Jerusalem had been torn down! Nehemiah could hardly bear the news about his beloved city. The holy city of David, the glory of Solomon's temple, and the place where the Lord's sacred presence had dwelt lay in ruins. His heart weighed heavy as he began to fast and pray, mourn and weep, before his God for days:

> "...Please, O Lord God of heaven, the great and awesome God, who keeps the covenant and lovingkindness for those who love Him and keep His commandments, please let Your ear be attentive and Your eyes open to hear the prayer of Your servant, which I am praying before You, day and night, on behalf of Your servants, the sons (descendants) of Israel (Jacob), confessing the sins of the sons of Israel which we have committed against You; I and my father's house have sinned. We have acted very corruptly against You and have not

kept the commandments, nor the statutes, nor the ordinances which You commanded Your servant Moses. Please remember the word which You commanded Your servant Moses, saying, 'If you are unfaithful *and* violate your obligations to Me I will scatter you [abroad] among the peoples; but if you return to Me and keep My commandments and do them, though those of you who have been scattered are in the most remote part of the heavens, I will gather them from there and will bring them to the place where I have chosen for My Name to dwell.' Now they are Your servants and Your people whom You have redeemed by Your great power and by Your strong hand. Please, O Lord, let Your ear be attentive to the prayer of Your servant and the prayer of Your servants who delight to [reverently] fear Your Name [Your essence, Your nature, Your attributes, with awe]; and make Your servant successful this day and grant him compassion in the sight of this man [the king]." Nehemiah 1:5–11 (Amplified)

Nehemiah was the cupbearer to King Artaxerxes. The cupbearer was in a very close and trusted position to the king, tasting and serving his wine. Up until this time, Nehemiah had not brought his personal feelings into his service for the king, but this day was different. The grief showed on his face and the king noticed it. Nehemiah was afraid.

When the king questioned him, Nehemiah fearfully disclosed the source of his grief. His explanation touched the king and he granted Nehemiah's request to return to his homeland to rebuild the walls of Jerusalem.

Why were the walls so important to Nehemiah when the whole city was devastated? The walls of the city represented its strength. The walls kept the enemy out and gave a high place for the watchmen to stand, foresee danger, and sound the alarm. In battle, the walls gave a fighting advantage by allowing those inside to look down on the approaching intruders. A sense of protection was given to those who lived within strong, well-built walls. The dignity of the city rested in its walls providing the ability to protect itself.

Today, the walls of protection around the church have been torn down. Those walls are strong doctrine that teach the truth concerning warfare against the approaching enemy. The walls of sound doctrine keep the enemy out, preserve the lives of the people who live within them, and provide for watchmen to recognize the enemy. Without the truth, God's people are unprotected from every wind of doctrine that carries them away from the solid rock, the Lord Jesus Christ.

The sledgehammer of religious tradition destroys those walls. People begin to lean on what looks familiar and comfortable instead of being alert to what is going on around them. Complacency sets in, the watchmen go to sleep, and the enemy moves in with no opposition. The exciting great adventure of following God becomes a lazy float down the river, just going with the flow. It is easy, and it is comfortable. It bores most people. God is exciting and always moving forward. To follow Him is to avoid being lulled into a deadly slumber by the enemy and ending up at the bottom of a waterfall.

Nehemiah did not move without prayer. God's people forget to pray when their relationship with Him becomes a ritual of tradition and man's religion. When we hear the word "church" today, it most likely is being used to describe a building where a pattern of behavior has been established. "Church" in the New Testament referred to a community of members on earth or saints in Heaven, or both, that had a personal relationship with God and heard His voice.

We have allowed rational thinking of man and the tactics of the enemy to remove the true nature of the church—intimacy with God and fellowship through love with other believers.

As truth about who we are in Christ, who Christ is in us, and the power that dwells with us and within us is taught to God's people once again, we rebuild the walls that have been torn down by a weak, powerless, watered-down doctrine.

The church has had a form of godliness but denied His power as truth gave way to society's demands. Purity has been lost in the church, and people wander through life without understanding because the pastors fear offending someone. Purity is power over Satan; it closes the door on attacks that could be devastating.

As Nehemiah's people worked to rebuild the wall, they held their weapon in one hand and worked with the other, Nehemiah 4:17. In other words, they were prepared for the attacks of the enemy, but it did not hinder their work. The Bible says they had a mind to work. They were ridiculed by the enemy, who said the wall would not stand: "If a fox walks on it, he will break down their stone wall," the enemy taunted.

When the walls of truth are once again being built around the church, do not expect numerous pats on the back. People will criticize the truth, and church people are the greatest critics, those who do not want to come out of comfortable, false beliefs. The walls are protection for God's people. It is instruction to guide and direct us into a successful future. Apostle Paul warned the church:

> "For I know this, that after my departing shall grievous wolves enter in among you, not sparing the flock. Also, of your own selves shall men arise, speaking perverse things, to draw away disciples after them."
> Acts 20:29–30

Nehemiah told the people not to be afraid of the enemy but to remember the Lord is great and mighty and to fight for your brothers, your sons and your daughters, your wives, and your houses.

We are fighting for the abundant life Jesus came to give us. We are fighting for truth. We must be aware of the enemy's tactics to destroy the truth that sets us free to live this abundant life. Why does the church have the same statistics as the world when it comes to suicide, divorce, unwed pregnancies, and other issues? Our walls have been torn down, the church has lost its dignity, and we lie in ruin and shame. What is really a tragedy is that most of the church does not recognize its own condition. Appearing similar to the world instead of being the shining light on a hill, the church fights to keep things the way they are instead of rebuilding. Today, the fight is against the truths of God instead of for them. The beautiful truth of redemption identifies that we have all sinned but when we turn to Christ we are washed as white as snow as if it never happened. We must call sin what it is, sin, so we can receive the washing of the blood of Jesus and be made new. There is new life for all those that repent.

Once again, we need to pick up the sword of the Spirit, the word of God, and live by it. We protect that which is holy as Jerusalem was holy. Discernment of good and evil comes when we know the truth and the enemy cannot creep in when we are unaware because he is recognized immediately by the Spirit of God in us.

> "Indeed, the question came up only because some men who pretended to be brothers had been sneaked in—they came in surreptitiously (secretly) to spy out the freedom we have in the Messiah Yeshua, so that they might enslave us. Not even for a minute did we give in to them, so that the truth of the Good News might be preserved for you." Galatians 2:4–5 (Complete Jewish Bible)

The Gospel, the word of God, is good news. If we do not know the truth, we fight against it and give support to the enemy, who carries tradition and religion of man that makes the flesh in us feel comfortable and seek the approval of men. The church must be prepared to secure the walls of protection with instruction, correction, and discipline in love by teaching the truth of God's word:

> "All scripture is given by inspiration of God, and is profitable for doctrine, for reproof, for

correction, for instruction in righteousness."
2 Timothy 3:16

God has not changed. He still lovingly guides and directs His own.

Despite attempts to be loving, there will be those who leave angry. Would you rather people leave angry or have God's presence leave? We desire the presence of God in His house more than we desire the approval of men.

Many Christians will follow a lie, not being able to discern good from evil because of the religious system that has been set up in the church and lack of reading the word. In my own experience, I see that it was common practice to read the Bible all the way through once a year, or to at least make a practice to read from it every day. That was just four generations ago. Now, very few have read the entire Bible even once.

God's ways are not our ways and His thoughts are not our thoughts, so when truth comes, we reject it, thinking that it surely must not be right because it goes against our formal teaching. At first, God's truth will sound outlandish to us. As we put away denominational thinking, wrong teaching, and man's social-club mentality for the church, we will begin to walk by faith and not by sight, receiving the higher call meant for us. Love will flow, and power will be seen in the church once again. We will begin to have God's thoughts and His ways.

To rebuild the walls, we must be armed as Nehemiah's men. Our weapons are the sword of the Spirit and the word of God. Knowing the truth exposes Satan's lies; he hates the truth. Speaking God's word establishes the truth and moves Heaven:

"Bless the LORD, ye his angels, that excel
in strength, that do his commandments,
hearkening unto the voice of his word."
Psalms 103:20

The angels are just waiting for us to speak the word God has given us. They listen for it and then perform it, hearkening. It is our voice speaking God's word in love that causes Heaven to move.

<u>Praise</u>, the high praises of God in our mouth with His word, defeats the enemy. God dwells in the praises of His people. Praise lifts heaviness and oppression and lets us see our circumstances more clearly.

<u>Submission to God and Resistance to the Devil</u>, obeying God's word strengthens us and destroys Satan's plans. Obedience and accepting God's ways in our lives brings wisdom, protection, and favor. As we resist the temptation to take the easy way out, that everyone is taking, we are telling the enemy, "No, I will not follow you," and he must flee.

<u>Faith</u> gives us the ability to stand when we look like we should be falling. Our shield of faith quenches every fiery dart of criticism, fear, doubt, and unbelief. Faith works by love and loving God, knowing God, causes us to want to do His will no matter how hard it is or what anyone else says or thinks.

<u>Love</u> covers a multitude of sins and destroys strife. Love never fails. It gives strength to the weary. Perfect love removes all fear. Our passionate love for God, our family, God's people, and the truth will keep us moving forward regardless of any opposition.

<u>Forgiveness</u> sets us free from tormenting anger and bitterness. It also sets others free. As we forgive others, the Father forgives us.

<u>Prayer</u>, being alone with God, and listening to His voice brings peace, revelation, and wisdom. We expect God to talk to us, so we listen:

> "My sheep hear my voice, and I know them,
> and they follow me." John 10:27

The zeal Jesus had for the house of God ate Him up, consumed Him. When the money-changers used the temple for their own agenda, He made a whip and drove them out. Satan always comes in with his own agenda for the people of God; his ideas, tactics, and manipulation. We must protect that which is holy. The words of Paul concerning the wolves have all but been forgotten and swept under the rug. Making a whip is not for us today, but Jesus does demonstrate to us His passion for holiness and truth. Speaking the truth in love is the passion for the church.

Remember that the people Satan is using are usually not even aware of what is being done with them, and true Christians are brothers and sisters in Christ. The enemy we want to drive out is the devil. His influence on people and the church is what will not be tolerated. Speaking the truth in love will set the captives free. God spoke to me these words concerning those used by the enemy: *Your job is to love them. My job is to change them.*

A woman who had attended our church called for me to come pray for her daughter in the hospital. The daughter's finger was infected and was not responding to antibiotics. The doctors were considering amputation. When I finished praying and talking with her daughter, the mother walked out behind me. She began to say, over and over, "I hate you. I hate you. I have prayed about this, but I still hate you." I kept walking, with her following behind me, a little embarrassed because of the hospital personnel that could hear her. I could not help but laugh because the devil was so blatantly exposing himself. I turned and looked her in the eye and lovingly said, "No, we love each other; we are God's children. This is the enemy, this is not you." I hugged her. She started all over again, "No, I hate you. I really do." I could not help but laugh as I tried to reason with her, but nothing changed her. The woman's husband came to church the next service and enthusiastically testified that His daughter was healed after the prayer. He was so excited. The mother never came back to church.

We will help multitudes when we do not compromise God's word. God's power will come into the church like never seen before when He sees He can trust us to protect His word. This can only be done with God's supernatural love pouring through us for Him, His word, and His people, therefore, we need to consult His Holy Spirit, His Spirit of Love, for all instruction, correction, and reproof.

When instruction comes from the flesh, it will not be what is needed to help, but it will hinder. Instruction from the Spirit is done with wisdom from above—which is first pure, then peaceable, easy to be entreated, merciful, without hypocrisy and partiality. Recognize who the true enemy is—Satan. Love the people, even when some will walk away. They did it to Jesus.

We are called to serve each other in love and to forbear one another, have patience and faith that God is working as the truth is being preached and acted out.

The rebuilding of the walls, the true doctrine of God, will bring back to the church her dignity, the power of God, and the purity of holiness. She will once again shine as a bright light in a dark world, leading men to the truth. There is grace for the church to walk in love and uncompromising truth:

"But thou, O Lord, art a God full of compassion, and gracious, longsuffering, and plenteous in mercy and truth." Psalms 86:15

Chapter 16
Humility, the Way Up

"When pride cometh, then cometh shame: but with the lowly is wisdom." Proverbs 11:2

I asked God, "What is pride?" Immediately, faster than I could write, came the answer. An endless list scrolled in front of my spiritual eyes of what we consider are natural human emotions. The list included most of our anger, sorrow, grief, self-pity, self-consciousness, timidity, anxiety, fear, stress, and on and on, much more than I can remember. I was surprised. The Lord revealed how most of our emotions are pride because we are egocentric, overly concerned about how we are affected. Maybe, we did not get our way, or we feel someone violated our rights. Very seldom do we have true righteous indignation or godly sorrow. Our emotions commonly stem from inconvenience.

Early in my ministry, I traveled to Texas to give my testimony with a group of women who were more seasoned than I. We had to take a twenty-four-hour Greyhound bus trip to get there from Florida because one of the women was afraid to fly. "Okay," I thought, "I can do this." God had opened the door for me to speak and I needed to go, so let the humbling begin.

As I attempted to be my well-taught, polite, conscientious self, some of the bus riders were quite gruff and I felt inadequate for the setting, like a fish out of water. It was approximately forty-eight hours round-trip—*joy*. I did manage to fall asleep for a short time. We were on our way to Texas when I had a dream that God was taking me out into the wilderness as He did with Elijah. The wilderness in the spirit is usually an uncomfortable place of humbling. God takes care of us in the wilderness even though we feel deserted. Just as Elijah was hated by the evil queen Jezebel, God also pointed out a leader in my life who hated me back home. "Hate" was such a strong word, it was unnerving to think that someone could hate me. When I woke up, I remember sighing, knowing I had no choice but to totally depend on God. I settled in for whatever this trip would bring. This was not the life I had planned.

I was new to ministering, but God worked through me as I spoke and touched hearts in one of the large Texas cowboy services. One minister told me, "You are humble." I smiled. What choice did I have? There I was, obeying God to speak, riding a bus for twenty-four hours with another trip to come. The women I was with were more polished and experienced. I felt like a child waiting to be told what to do next as we went from one ministry setting to another. It was a long week. God had a plan for me in each setting. It was good, just so incredibly uncomfortable and, at times, irritating. I did not feel very Christlike, so I kept my mouth shut as much as possible.

Finally, we were on our way home. I endured the hostile bus environment and looked forward to getting back. Our last bus finally arrived at home. We all waited for our luggage. When mine did not come out with the others', tracing it revealed my luggage had been sent to New York instead of Florida. Through gritted teeth and tense muscles, I took a deep breath. This trip had been more than humbling; it was crucifying, and God was in it all. I think He was laughing.

Why would we even want humility when it seems all the world is looking for the opposite? Pats on the back, exaltation, praise, recognition, and honor are the things that man is seeking. We humble ourselves to do God's will because the child of God has a desire to please God and to hear Him say, "Well, done, my good and faithful servant." We do not realize how self-centered we are until we look at the life of Jesus.

> "For thus saith the high and lofty One that inhabiteth eternity, whose name is Holy; I dwell in the high and holy place, with him also that is of a contrite and humble spirit, to revive the spirit of the humble, and to revive the heart of the contrite ones." Isaiah 57:15

There we have it—humility. That is the way we reach the top, the high place, the holy place, the place of glorious fellowship and loving relationship with our most beloved Father. It is not the world's way; it is His way.

> "Humble yourselves therefore under the mighty hand of God, that He may exalt you in due time." 1 Peter 5:6

There is the true exalting man is seeking. Notice the "due time" part. There is no definite time specified, so this could seem to take forever. Humbling ourselves to accept the will of God in our lives and His loving chastening may not sound like the thrill of a lifetime, but it is, because it yields the peaceable fruit of righteousness, and that righteousness takes us to places with God we never imagined. He can bless us with the fruit of His Spirit; righteousness, peace, and joy. In this high place, we can walk with peace while everyone is stressed out. We become accustomed to being guided by the Holy Spirit and we wait patiently to hear His voice. Fear is overcome by faith. We learn to depend on God and not ourselves. Our circumstances begin to change. It all starts with humility.

Continuing to hear and obey God, we fall more and more in love with Him. He directs us, and we begin to see the good of it, not just the pain. He is gently transforming us into the image of His Son. He patiently waits for us to stop kicking and screaming, then moves to the next phase.

"...Before honor is humility." Proverbs 18:12.

"By humility and the fear of the LORD are
riches, and honor, and life." Proverbs 22:4

The way up is down, or so it seems with God. He looks for those with pure hearts, those who just want what He wants. When we see pride, the Bible says destruction is on the way. When we see humility, honor is coming. We can ask God to reveal any pride in us; we are usually blinded to our own faults.

The world overlooks the meek, the humble, the gentle and quiet spirit, which is of valuable to God. In time, *due time*, God will exalt this person, lift them up out of the rubble and people will wonder, "Where did they come from?" God knows how to exalt His people. He knows how to bring honor to the humble.

Esther was a Jewish girl, unknown until she was chosen as queen and used as a savior for her people. It was David, a simple shepherd boy who God used to kill the giant Goliath. A lowly stable housed the birth of the great I Am.

God delights in using the simple things to confuse the wise and the weak things of this earth to astound the mighty. If we will allow God to take us to what seems to be the low places, He can do great things through us.

In the book *Humility* by Andrew Murray, he writes:

> "Humility, the place of entire dependence on God, is, from the very nature of things, the first duty and the highest virtue of the creature. In fact, it is the root of every virtue. And so pride, or the loss of this humility, is the root of every sin and evil!"[1]

We cannot obtain humility on our own; it will be given to us as we become more and more obedient to Christ, surrendering our will to His. When we feel those urgings and promptings from the Holy Spirit, instead of ignoring them, we obey them. We come out of our complacency (self-satisfaction) and shed off pride. It can be agonizing at first, but the more we follow God, the more we will become comfortable in the lower places until He exalts us, brings us to better things. We must admit that some of our deepest beliefs are wrong and change our way of thinking. We may have to apologize to someone when they were more in the wrong than ourselves. These are emotionally painful pride killers. As the Holy Spirit reveals what is needed in our lives and we do it, we become clothed in humility, preparing ourselves to be empowered by the Father. Empowered to defeat the enemy.

Jesus calls us to serve one another. He demonstrated this to His disciples when He washed their feet. Serving others brings a joy that cannot come from any other lifestyle. It sets us free from ourselves and the pride that hinders our walk with God. Serving puts the focus on others and not us.

Heaven's acceptance and enthusiasm for others will be alive in us, we will be Christ on earth, laying down our lives for the people of God.

Strange as it may seem, the lower we stoop to help others, the greater the joy that springs up in us. It is the high road that few have found. It is the path of life that delivers us from our tormenting self.

Paul recounted how he served the Lord with all lowliness and tears, even afflictions from his own people. He did not stop declaring what was truth and good for all who would listen. He taught publicly as well as from house to house the way of salvation through Jesus Christ our Lord. He would follow the leading of the Holy Spirit even though it was made known to him that more trials and afflictions awaited him. He did not count his life for anything but to do the work of the ministry and the calling God had given him. He wanted to finish his course testifying of the Gospel of the grace of God.

Paul prayed for the Ephesians to have revelation in the knowledge of Jesus and that they would know the exceeding greatness of His power. This power is in us to overcome the flesh and Satan in our lives. To pray for others causes us to care for them more, putting ourselves aside.

The natural fleshly mind tries to rationalize (sounds almost like "rational lies") not serving God. The Spirit gives instruction contrary to the flesh. We think of ourselves first, but God tells us to put others first.

Humbling ourselves toward God's people is the real proof that we are truly humble souls. Cowering, fear of man, or being beaten down is not humility and neither is false humility. True humility is strength, defying self-preservation, and counts others as important, no matter who they are. Our humility is gentle with those who are weak. We do not get offended because we love God and we love His Word.

Paul had lost sight of himself. His eyes were on the work of the Lord Jesus Christ. What man did to him was of no importance; it did not move him. His humility had taken his eyes off himself and his own sufferings to put them on the building of the church and the prize that lay ahead, the Lord Jesus Christ.

May we, too, take our eyes off ourselves and put them on Jesus and His people He has set before us to love and serve. God made it very clear concerning people when He said to me, *"Your job is to love them. My job is to change them."* That has made my life easier. I have not had to convince anyone of anything, nor defend myself. I have had to ask for more love multiple times and, of course, God's grace has always supplied.

God made it so real to me that without humility none of us are going anywhere with Him. As Moses prayed, so did I:

"And Moses said to Him, "If Your presence
does not go [with me], do not lead us up from
here. For how then can it be known that Your
people and I have found favor in Your sight?
Is it not by Your going with us, so that we
are distinguished, Your people and I, from all
the [other] people on the face of the earth?"
Exodus 33:15–16 (Amplified)

God's presence lets us know we have found grace in His sight. We want Him above all things. Grace is what separates, or sets apart, God's people as being different from the world.

I read Andrew Murray's little book, *Humility, the Pocket Companion,* over and over, even making it one of my continual go-to books year after year. I gave every member of my congregation a copy as we studied it to recognize and seek deliverance from our own pride.

Humbling and trying times in life have not been wasted. They are for testing and proving, strengthening and establishing. There is coming a raising up of the humble and an exalting of the righteous. His promises are true.

Chapter 17

The Holy Spirit, the Spirit of Grace

"And the scripture was fulfilled which saith, Abraham believed God, and it was imputed unto him for righteousness: and he was called the Friend of God." James 2:23

Our relationship with the Holy Spirit of God is so very precious. It is through the Holy Spirit that we are taught the Word of God, for He is the teacher. He brings to our remembrance the things we have learned just when we need them. He causes us to understand supernaturally, unlike human knowledge, and He is our Comforter.

He brings wisdom that precludes believers from experiencing life as others do—which is living without the benefit of the Holy Spirit's discernment. Instead of becoming outraged at some slanderous thing said about us, we begin to pray for that one who spoke out against us, realizing the judgment they have brought on themselves. Even turmoil and crises are met with peace when our Divine Comforter engulfs us in His grace. This mind-set can only come from a Spirit of love and wisdom. He brings that wisdom from above, which is first pure, then peaceable, gentle, and kind, easy to obey, full of mercy and good fruits, without partiality and without hypocrisy, James 3:17.

> "I have many more things to say to you, but you cannot bear [to hear] them now. But when He, the Spirit of Truth, comes, He will guide you into all the truth [full and complete truth]. For He will not speak on His own initiative, but He will speak whatever He hears [from the Father—the message regarding the Son], and He will disclose to you what is to come [in the future]." John 16:12–13 (Amplified)

The Spirit speaking to us gives truth that strengthens and encourages, giving hope for the future. All the world can offer is sympathy without true understanding. God gives understanding and a future plan, revealing that whatever we are experiencing is bringing that plan into our lives. We do not respond like the world because the Holy Spirit opens our heart to His way of seeing things.

The Holy Spirit gives gifts to men and divides them as He will. The gifts are of the Spirit, so He is the One that helps us understand how to use them and have discernment with them. All these things that He does are to guide us into all truth, that we might be more like Jesus.

Our gifts are not for us; they are for others to see and know Christ. We are spent for His glory alone, surrendered vessels through which His power flows. What joy and peace come from completely yielding to His will.

> "The grace of the Lord Jesus Christ, and the love
> of God, and the communion of the Holy Ghost,
> be with you all. Amen." II Corinthians 13:14

Communion, intimate fellowship with the Holy Spirit, is the privilege we have as Christ's followers. God desires relationship with His people and His Spirit is the One that is present on earth to communicate with us and testify of the Lord Jesus Christ. The Holy Spirit brings the presence of the Father and the Son. As we spend time in the Lord's presence, we will hear His voice more and more in our spirit.

> "The Spirit Himself testifies *and* confirms
> together with our spirit [assuring us] that
> we [believers] are children of God." Romans
> 8:16 (Amplified)

When we believe in the Lord Jesus Christ as our Savior, then we are sealed with the Holy Spirit of promise. It is like a king putting his signet in the hot wax to seal a letter. His signet, the Holy Spirit, comes to seal us and identify us as His own.

The Holy Spirit is not an "it" and not a force. The Holy Spirit is a person. He has the attributes of a person, a list I heard from another minister:

He speaks, Revelation 2:7.
He intercedes, Romans 8:26.
He testifies, John 15:26.

He leads, Acts 8:29.
He commands, Acts 16:6, 7.
He guides, John 16:13.
He can be lied to, Acts 5:34.
He can be insulted, Matthew 12:31, 32.
He can be grieved, Ephesians 4:30.
He is called Eternal Spirit, Hebrews 9:14.
He is everywhere, Psalms 139:7.
He is all knowing, 1 Corinthians 2:10-11.
He is called God, Acts 5:3, 4.

> "We are to no longer live by the flesh but by the Spirit." Romans 8:1

> "For in him we live, and move, and have our being..." Acts 17:28

His urgings and promptings guide us through life, as well as, words that are spoken directly to our spirit. When we acknowledge God, stop and listen throughout the day to what He is speaking to us, our steps will be ordered by the Lord with peace.

The Holy Spirit is a supernatural power working in us to lay hands on the sick and see them healed, to speak to a problem and see it resolved, to walk in righteousness and refuse evil, to prosper spiritually and physically. He directs us to Jesus, our wonderful, loving Savior. He strengthens us in the inner man and reveals truth. The Holy Spirit is the Spirit of Grace in us to live the Christ centered life.

Chapter 18
A Virtuous Woman

"Who can find a virtuous woman? For her
price [is] far above rubies." Proverbs 31:10

Proverbs 31 describes the virtuous woman, she is priceless. She spins cloth. She gets up in the middle of the night and fixes food for everyone in the house. She has strength and honor, wisdom and kindness. She dresses great and her husband has a voice in the land. Is there such a person? Yes! Those who trust in the Lord and love righteousness are clothed with strength. Honor is given to the ones who are spiritually strong enough not to exalt themselves but have confidence in knowing who they are in Christ. The Lord will exalt them. Wisdom is for all who will simply ask of the Lord.

The word "virtuous" is used in this verse for the original Hebrew word in the Old Testament *chayil,* meaning "strength, might, ability, wealth, army, force."[2] No matter what has been done or happened in the life of a child of

God, the blood of Christ has washed it clean. Knowing we are now the righteous children of God and living the virtuous life brings strength and power.

We cower under our failures, when we could have done better and did not. The Lord spoke to me in prayer one morning: "*I am not counting your failures, I am counting your victories.*" God is not looking at your faults; He is searching the depths of your heart for just a little faith, a little hope, a little love:

> "...the smoking flax He will not quench...,"
> Isaiah 42:3

Even if you are not on fire with passion for Him now, the little smoke coming from your heart that searches for Him draws Him to you.

Our righteousness is not of ourselves, it is—and has always been, from God. We feel like we do not measure up because we see our faults and failures. God knew about our faults and failures long before they ever happened. He gave the supreme sacrifice, Jesus Christ, to pay for them. Our virtue is in Him. We are His and He gives us Christ's holiness as we walk with Him. We are virtuous and blameless in His sight!

Look what you have been through to make it this far! Life gets rough—you have stood the test of time and you are still standing. There is fortitude, personal bravery, and strength to keep going and overcome. You have probably been through more than most know. Most likely, you have gotten up, brushed yourself off, and kept going more times than you can count. You are strength personified in

Christ! Everyone does not see it, but your Father does. He is delighted in you!

> "A virtuous woman is a crown to her husband..." Proverbs 12:4

The Bible tells us that God said it was not good for man to be alone. Women bring strength to a relationship to see beyond what is happening now. Men need the powerful supernatural hope that is in a woman's heart to see beyond the problem and to the solution. The two of them together bring strength to each other and forge ahead in life to accomplish what could seem impossible.

The heart of a mother is toward her children as the heart of God is toward His children. The older women who have persevered for their families, living with the struggles of everyday life, have wisdom to teach the younger women. It is the duty of the older women to mentor the younger and not get so caught up in their own lives. This is so desperately needed today. Young women are having children with no idea how to guide them or how to fight to keep their family together against an enemy that wants to tear them apart. Older women, you are needed! Every stage of womanhood is incredibly important to the Kingdom of God. A new grace comes with each phase of life.

A meek and quiet spirit in the sight of God is of a great price, 1 Peter 3:4. Meekness is characterized by patience and long-suffering, not weakness. Meekness is strength undercover. This gives the family stability when the mother can remain patient and long-suffering in trying times. It is a strength that does not have to prove itself. This very present fortitude develops healthy minds in the children and security to know that whatever is happening around us, Mom is there.

The wife who remains stable and does not lose her faith in God—especially when everything in her is crying out "It's a lost cause!"—gives her husband strength to keep going. A help-meet, Genesis 1:18, one fit for the service, does not agree with the enemy, the outward circumstances, or the voice of defeat but looks to Jesus, the author and finisher of our faith. She stands in the day of battle, a pillar of strength to the household. Behind closed doors, she will be on her knees pouring out her heart to God, the One who gives her strength. There may be tears when alone, but with others, she gives words of encouragement. She has learned to encourage herself, regardless as to whether anyone else does or not.

How can she do this? She rises while it is yet night. She gathers manna from above, feeds on what Heaven has to offer, and then carries it out with all that are in her house. She relies on God, even when her efforts seem like they are not making a difference, because she knows that He has not forgotten her or her family. Her prayers have cost her meals, sleep, and pleasure. They have been a sacrifice to her God, and yet at the same time a delight, knowing she does not carry the burden of her family, her Heavenly Father does. In all her shortcomings, impatience, and useless human per-fectionism, He is watching, protecting, comforting, and per-fecting that which concerns her.

Strength and honor are her clothing, and she is thrilled about her family's future. She knows her children are taught of the Lord and covered in the scarlet blood of Jesus. Wisdom is in her mouth and the law of kindness is on her tongue because being with her Father has filled her with the Holy Spirit working to yield the fruit of love, joy, peace, long-suffering, goodness, faith, meekness, and temperance. When she loses it, she brings her emotions back under control and waits for her time to come. Continuous persistence in self-control brings her wisdom and strength:

> "...in quietness and in confidence shall be your strength..." Isaiah 30:15

This strong and courageous woman speaks encouragement to her husband and children. After about fourteen years of marriage, I finally learned men need our praise. They need to know that what they do for us matters. I came home from work one day, exhausted beyond words. As I walked into the living room, I saw my sons watching their dad, Donald, putting a new door on the hall closet, something Donald knew I had wanted for about a year. It was a difficult fit and I knew he had worked hard on it. He was so proud. "Look, honey!" He opened and closed the door to demonstrate how well it worked. I knew this was a pivotal moment; what I said or did was going to make an impact. It had to be good. Mental fatigue from a twelve-hour-long night shift working ICU had blocked all creativity. I responded the best that I could with what cognition I had left. "Honey, look at you! Look what you can do! I'm so proud of you!" My Sesame Street–style rhyme left the boys in stitches, mockingly repeating my words through their laughter. "Yeah, Dad, Look at you! Look what you can do! I'm so proud of you!"

Truly, my thankfulness for the closet door was sincere and Donald knew it. We used the praise chant for years when someone did anything worth noting.

I had to make a choice, come in irritable and go straight to bed or try to engage and be positive. I'm glad I pulled myself together for my family.

The virtuous woman knows she is not perfect and the repented-of mistakes in her life do not negate her significance in God's kingdom. She is raising mighty warriors for the battles of life, she gives them confidence with grace. Pain, hurt, and past mistakes have no toll on her as she replaces them with the task at hand, to keep her home stable no matter what the world's atmosphere.

This woman guards her heart and her mouth from wrong words. She reaches out to help others without judging. She is intelligent and creative. She is not idle, and her family recognizes her worth, maybe not always, but they will. God is with her. The fatigue of home, job, and the world may weigh heavily on her at times, but God's Word reaffirms that He is ordering her steps. She trusts Him. In all her faults and fears, her heart longs for Him and searches for Him.

To say that grace covers this woman in all her ways, I believe, is an understatement. I would say abundant grace is poured out on her and she is a delight to the Lord. Is she perfect? Not to herself and the world, but to God, yes, through the blood of Jesus. Virtuous? Yes, Her Father has made her so. He sees no fault in her.

Chapter 19

Spiritual Warfare

We are at war! There is a battle raging, and we are in it. The problem is many Christians are unaware of the danger. As a supernatural, demonic spirit-led army wreaks havoc on our minds, families, churches, communities, nation, and especially our children, we have sat back with no retaliation and let the devil have what is ours. As born-again, blood-bought saints of God, we have been given authority to use the name of Jesus and take down what is happening around us. Complacency has lulled the church to sleep while the enemy has blatantly walked into the camp and taken all he wanted.

The great thing about this war is that we are on the winning side! It is a fixed fight:

> "When He had disarmed the rulers and author-
> ities [those supernatural forces of evil oper-
> ating against us], He made a public example
> of them [exhibiting them as captives in His
> triumphal procession], having triumphed

over them through the cross." Colossians 2:15 (Amplified)

It is a spiritual entity that is controlling ranks and ranks of an invisible army that plots and plans to steal, kill, and destroy. We are to stand up, war as good soldiers, remove the enemy from the camp, and then go to his camp, the darkness, and take back the stolen goods, the precious souls imprisoned in hopelessness.

We have been given mighty and powerful weapons of warfare. First, we renew our minds for the confrontation. We cast down every imagination that is against the ways of God, such as:
"My situation is never going to change."
"I'm not good enough to be used by God. I'm too old, young, sinful, dumb, unskilled, etc."

Satan is an accuser of God's people, the Bible says. We can ask the Holy Spirit to search our hearts and minds, expose any lie the enemy had told us, and remove it. When jealousy, envy, anger, bitterness, rebellion, fear, doubt, or unbelief are exposed, we confess them to God and surrender our will to His. Hit each one with the Word of God to annihilate the lies that agree with those entities.

This enemy we war against in our minds is the same enemy that terrorized our nation on 9/11. It is the same enemy that convinced my son to kill himself. It is the same enemy that has attempted to take my life on several occasions and the lives of many others of God's people. He wants nothing less than to murder those who follow God's word. Jesus said he was a murderer from the beginning. He desires to take us down a road of destruction, to torment and to oppress. He is the spirit of terrorism.

A young man from our church who was serving in the army was stationed in Iraq. The Taliban had been threatening to kill his men for days. He was able to contact me through the Internet. The night before, he was awakened by a dark entity that came into his tent and began to attack him in his bed. It was not human, but he felt the pressure of it as it tried to snuff out his life. He was finally able to speak the name of Jesus and it left. I told him what the Lord was revealing to me. It was the spirit of the devil that he and his men were fighting. Though they were fighting physically, there was a spiritual evil, satanic force behind the Taliban. I told him to plead the blood of Jesus over him and his men. Command the demons to go, in Jesus' name and pray Psalm 91 for protection.

Satan takes authority by using illegitimate means; his authority has been stripped from him by Jesus Christ. When we take our God-given rightful authority over Satan, he must leave.

> "Submit yourselves therefore, to God; Resist
> the devil and he will flee from you." James 4:7

Sometimes our submission to God may cost us our time, dignity, and pride. We submit to what God tells us even if we do not understand why we are doing it. I was given gold teardrop earrings by a friend and told that the Lord wanted me to have them because of the tears I would shed for the people. I wondered, "What tears?"

One day, God told me to pray on my face in front of the church I was attending before I became a pastor. I was to pray for the people of that church that they would be spared. I did not know why I had to get on my face in front of all those people before the service began, neither did I know why I was praying to spare them, nor did I know from what they needed to be spared, but I did it.

Shortly after, when we had to leave that church, I did not cry for me and my family, my heart was for the people who did not understand. I was afraid the people were not spared. I cried those tears God said I would shed for the people. Through those prayers, He preserved individuals for His purpose. My submission to His voice had spared them from the enemy's attacks. I was put in a position to lead those people even before I knew it.

In our warfare, we are not coming against people, even though they are the ones that are being led by the enemy, but we are coming against spiritual wickedness. We have the power of the Holy Spirit in us to pray for people who the devil is controlling and see God set them free:

> "Ye are of God, little children, and have over-
> come them: because greater is he that is in
> you, than he that is in the world." 1 John 4:4.

God uses the enemy to refine us. Our battles are strengthening, teaching, and purifying us for His Kingdom's work:

> "For the time being no discipline brings joy,
> but seems sad *and* painful; yet to those
> who have been trained by it, afterwards it
> yields the peaceful fruit of righteousness
> [right standing with God and a lifestyle and

attitude that seeks conformity to God's will
and purpose]." Hebrews 12:11 (Amplified)

Because God loves us, He prepares us for our future to
be sent out into the world by allowing these skirmishes
with the devil to strengthen us:

"Then said Jesus to them again, Peace be unto
you: as my Father hath sent me, even so send
I you." John 20:21

We are His deputies with full authority, through prayer,
to uphold the divine will of God. The deputy is invested with
the full power of the office of his chief and is fully autho-
rized to act in his stead. Our mission is to be so yielded to
God that we know His heart in a matter, discerning truth,
and bringing that truth in love. Our prayers for others are
our mission to increase God's kingdom on earth. We are
sent out into the world to school, work, restaurants, or any
public or private place with God's mission to bring His light.

God looks for men and women who will stand in the gap,
give themselves to prayer and intercession for His people:

"And I sought for a man among them, that
should make up the hedge, and stand in the
gap before me for the land..." Ezekiel 22:30

God was looking for someone to pray for His people.
As the Lord led me to pray scripture, to take down the
motives of the enemy, there was one passage that was
highly effective:

"Blessed is the man that walketh not in the counsel of the ungodly, nor standeth in the way of sinners, nor sitteth in the seat of the scornful. But his delight is in the law of the LORD; and in his law doth he meditate day and night. And he shall be like a tree planted by the rivers of water, that bringeth forth his fruit in his season; his leaf also shall not wither; and whatsoever he doeth shall prosper." Psalm 1:1–3

I prayed this over myself and my husband many times through the years and saw real changes in both of us. There are many other scriptures to pray, especially in the book of Psalms.

Inserting our name or another person's name in these scriptures and reading them out loud is a powerful weapon against the enemy. It is called *decreeing*, and when we, as God's children, decree a thing—it is established:

"Thou shalt also decree a thing, and it shall be established unto thee: and the light shall shine upon thy ways." Job 22:28

It was praying the scripture, as prompted by the Holy Spirit, that led me into God's truth following Andy's death. It brought peace, strength, deliverance, and power into my life. The more I prayed the word of God, the more I understood Him and His ways. I became intimate with God praying what He said about me in His word.

Standing on the Word, believing and speaking, is a spiritual sword in our hand, loosening the grip of the devil from people's souls, our own included. I have seen this work, setting the captives free from all sorts of demonic strongholds, such as: suicide, pornography, fear, and more. We must see those for whom the prayer is being said as set free even before it happens. That is faith at work.

It is not just repeating words but a heartfelt reception of the truth knowing God said it, and therefore it is true. Getting it down in our spirit and living the life He meant for us to live.

As we hear God's voice, He will give us what I call *genius battle tactics*. These will be words to speak, prayers to pray, actions to take, or people to confront lovingly, in a way that has not entered our mind. When we carry out those battle tactics, they will have purpose and power. Odd as they may seem at times, God is a brilliant commander in chief. He paid a high price for our victory; He wants to see us win and overcome everything the devil has thrown at us:

> "To him that overcometh will I grant to sit with me in my throne, even as I also overcame, and am set down with my Father in his throne." Revelation 3:21

Prayer overcomes the evil that tries to lure our flesh into union with Satan's plans and his destruction for our lives and others.

God wants us to reign and rule with Christ. Prayer is acting with authority. This is God's plan for us to rule with Christ, He has given us dominion, rule, over the works of His hands:

"Thou madest him to have dominion over the
works of thy hands; thou hast put all [things]
under his feet." Psalm 8:6

When we decree the word of God, it is the prayer of
faith that accomplishes that word's purpose, and it will not
return void. Heaven is acting on it:

"Bless the Lord, ye His angels, that excel in
strength, hearkening unto the voice of His
word." Psalm 103:20

When we speak and pray the word of God, we are the
voice of His word sending out the angel armies to do the
will of God. It is powerful!

Chapter 20
Our Own Worst Enemy

I was asking God in prayer what spirit was our enemy, which one was trying to get into our congregation, and who had it, "Was it I, Lord?" The phrase came to me from a comic strip I had once read with a little guy standing on the bow of a ship looking out over the ocean saying, "I have seen the enemy and it is us." Shortly after that, I picked up a book to read and it happened to have the phrase in it. "We are our own worst enemy." Paul talks about his greatest struggle:

> "For I know that in me (that is, in my flesh,) dwelleth no good thing: for to will is present with me; but how to perform that which is good I find not. For I delight in the law of God after the inward man: But I see another law in my members, warring against the law of my mind, and bringing me into captivity to the law of sin which is in my members. O wretched man that I am! Who shall deliver me from the body of this death? I thank God through Jesus Christ our Lord. So then, with

the mind I myself serve the law of God; but with
the flesh the law of sin." Romans 7:18, 22–25

I heard a preacher say once, "Your flesh hates God." I
thought that sounded a little harsh, but to think carnally is:

"...the earthly nature of man apart from divine
influence..." Strong's Concordance [3]

The fleshly nature is enmity against God, Romans 8:7.
The flesh, with all its desires and lusts that are against
God, will be subdued and harnessed for the work of God's
kingdom as we walk in obedience. Those wrongful desires
are crucified with Christ as we follow Him more and more.
God is for us. He loves us. The flesh will lead us to destruction. The flesh, or carnal way of thinking, will unite with
Satan in robbing our spirit of all that God has given us—life,
and that with abundance!

Years ago, to be able to sit down with a plate of home-
made peanut butter fudge and a large glass of whole milk
was my idea of paradise. Today, many years later, I have
managed to subdue the flesh enough to trade the plate of
fudge for a plate of saltine crackers and a dish of sardines.
I was told by a nutritionist that to optimize my health I
needed to eat sardines regularly. God had already spoken
to me about eating more fish. At first, I could not look at
them, much less touch or eat them. I could not even open
the can. I had to get a man from our church who ate them
regularly to open the first one and eat it in front of me so I
would believe they were edible. I have come a long way to
be able to eat them multiple times a week.

It took changing my way of thinking and desiring the better outcome of tough discipline with determination. I have seen results and it is worth the cost. My carnal way of thinking was destructive. God's ways are restorative.

That is how it is with following Christ. Peace of mind, a relationship with the Father, supernatural guidance, and amazing hope for the future are worth the price of discipline over the words I say, the thoughts I think, and the choices I make in life.

Satan appeals to the flesh. The flesh demands to be comfortable and to have its appetites fed. The only way to life is to deny the flesh, take up the cross, the calling on our lives, of the Lord Jesus Christ, and follow Him. Our flesh will be used for carrying the Kingdom of God to the world—even through our children. Receiving God's will as our own leads to peace and we serve the Lord with gladness. It becomes a joy to do what God has for us.

In jail ministry, I held women in my arms as they wept over all they had lost with their children because of drugs, men, and jail time. The pain of following the flesh is not worth what it costs us:

> "But every man is tempted, when he is drawn
> away of his own lust, and enticed. Then, when
> lust hath conceived, it bringeth forth sin: and
> sin, when it is finished, bringeth forth death."
> James 1:14–15

We do it to ourselves when we go our own way, which is to follow the devil, instead of God's way. We kill our own peace and joy in the Lord. We head off down a dark road. Our flesh is weak. That is why we have a Savior.

God is so merciful to keep working with us until His plan is carried out in us. We can see He was making a way to bring us back to Him, even when we seemed so far off course.

God is so good to us. As I worked with the women in the jail, I spoke the hope of God into them. God not only puts us back on the right path, but He is a restorer.

> "And I will restore to you the years that the locust hath eaten..." Joel 2:25

In other words, God will take back what the devil has robbed during our down time and give it back to us—our joy, our peace, good relationships, and more. God can make the time we lost into new years with even greater blessings and greater relationships. The Lord spoke to me, "*My restoration is with multiplication.*" That is so awesome; more than we lost is given back to us. Now, that is grace!

Sometimes our loss is because we blew it; other times we were attacked because we were doing something right. Regardless of the reason, God is telling us because the enemy dared to touch His beloved son or daughter, our Father is going to prepare a banquet for us in the presence of our enemies. Amazing!

Everyday God gives us choices. He will give us guidance with those choices if we ask Him. This verse even gives us the answer to the multiple-choice decision:

> "...I have set before you life and death, blessing and cursing: therefore choose life, that both thou and thy seed may live."
> Deuteronomy 30:19

Jesus Christ has already defeated Satan at the cross. Walking in the abundant life that victory gives us means we believe we are victorious, blessed, loved by our Heavenly Father, and that we have a great cloud of witnesses, including our friends and family members, cheering us on. All of Heaven wants to see us win!

To live in the spirit is to follow the ways of God when no one else will, because it is the path to life. To live in the flesh is to appease all those around us, as well as our own flesh. It is the way to death—spiritual death. We have power in us that the world does not know. That is the power of the Holy Spirit. The Amplified Bible describes it like this:

> "immeasurable *and* unlimited *and* surpassing greatness of His [active, spiritual] power is in us who believe." Ephesian 1:19 (Amplified)

God has given us everything we need to overcome our carnal nature, choose life, and live abundantly for Him!

Chapter 21

Spirit, Soul, and Body

"There is a spirit in man; and the inspiration of the Almighty giveth them understanding." Job 32:8

The Father is looking for those that worship Him in spirit and in truth. The Bible tells us to walk in the spirit. Our journey of following God and His ways brings us to love Him more and more, drawing us to give Him heartfelt praise for His goodness. That praise draws us even closer to Him, causing Him to draw closer to us, bringing us into a place of total submission to Him. His presence becomes evident. Worship begins as His love engulfs us and we pour it back out to Him. We adore Him.

We know our physical bodies get us around in this world and give us perception of what is happening by sight, hearing, touch, smell, and taste. Without these senses, it becomes a little more difficult to operate in our environment. Our body can be a distraction to us as we try to still the soul and focus on the Lord. The psalmist prayed:

"Teach me Thy way, O LORD; I will walk in
Thy truth: unite my heart to fear Thy name."
Psalms 86:11

Our heart is divided between God and the worldly desires. In subduing the flesh and opening our heart, we will find His presence more and more.

Beyond the physical body, there is a soul. In this realm of the soul are the mind and the heart, not the physical organs but the thought processes of man. These thoughts are born out of what we are taught from the time we are born. In other words, what people have spoken into us, such as our parents, TV, friends, teachers, music lyrics, etc. influence us.

Thoughts are formed by our carnal perception of people and things around us. We, also, have an enemy that thrives on putting thoughts in our mind to confuse and destroy the handiwork of God, His people. As these thoughts progress, our hearts are formed and attitudes are developed. Without being a child of God, a person would not have the Holy Spirit in him to speak truth to his heart and mind; therefore, he would become a product of these other voices.

The soul is where we react according to our preconceived notions and what we have been taught. We must deprogram our thought life that has come from the outside and reprogram our thoughts with the Holy Spirit's truth. This is contrary to what we thought we knew.

Ephesians 4:23 tells us to be renewed in the spirit of our minds. This is done when we have accepted Christ as our Savior and begin to feed on His Word. The innermost part of man is the spirit, which comes alive in us when we receive Christ as our Savior and Lord. Once we begin to live for Christ, we can then take over the soul, our emotions and actions, by removing the falsehoods and misconceptions of the world, our own erroneous thoughts, and the lies of the enemy, as we replace them with truth. The truth enters us by putting His Word in our heart. The wrong voices have fed us for too long. We need a washing, and the Word of God washes our hearts and minds.

> "...Christ also loved the church and gave him-
> self for it; That He might sanctify and cleanse
> it with the washing of water by the word."
> Ephesians 5:25–26

As we know more of God's Word, our discernment for truth is sharpened. We begin to walk, not by what we hear with our physical ears or what we see with our physical eyes, what people around us say, or the negative thoughts of the enemy, but by what God is speaking to us through His Word. We are beginning to walk in the spirit.

We can know what is from God regarding the thoughts and intentions of our own hearts and minds. That discernment comes from reading the Word of God and listening to the Holy Spirit:

> "For the word of God is quick [living] and pow-
> erful, and sharper than any two-edged sword,
> piercing even to the dividing asunder of soul
> and spirit, and of the joints and marrow, and

is a discerner of the thoughts and intents of
the heart." Hebrews 4:12

The Word of God divides what has been received in
our soul from what God reveals to us by the spirit. While
reading the Bible, some scripture jumps out and we know
that scripture is for us. It will reveal something we knew in
our spirit that is truth from Heaven, or it can reveal something from our own thinking that needs to go. This revelation through dividing truth from fiction will always move
us to a good place spiritually. He is the one that reveals the
truth about us to us:

"And he that searcheth the hearts knoweth
what is the mind of the spirit, because he
maketh intercession for the saints according
to the will of God." Romans 8:27

The Psalmist cried out to be delivered from secret faults,
asking, "Who can understand his errors?" Spirit must reveal
spirit. In our own carnal minds, we are helpless to know
much truth even about ourselves. We must have the Holy
Spirit reveal our hearts to us to know where we need to
change our actions and ways of thinking.

The Lord says:

"For my thoughts are not your thoughts, neither are your ways my ways." Isaiah 55:8

By His Holy Spirit's teaching, we know His thoughts and
His ways that we might live a blessed life.

To worship God, we advance past the physical body, proceeding on, bypassing the soul (what we think or feel), and going on to the spirit. There we will find the fellowship we all long to have with our Lord, Spirit to spirit. Quietly, we still our soul to hear from Him, all darkness fades away. In the description of a place where no demonic force can find, we get some understanding to spiritual contact with God:

> "There is a path which no fowl knoweth, and which the vulture's eye hath not seen: "... But where shall wisdom be found? [and where is] the place of understanding? Man knoweth not the price thereof; neither is it found in the land of the living. ... It cannot be gotten for gold, neither shall silver be weighed [for] the price thereof. ...God understandeth the way thereof, and he knoweth the place thereof."
> Job 28:7, 12–13, 15, and 23

Man cannot find that spiritual place with God except that he surrender his will to the Holy Spirit in becoming still before the Lord. It is the place where the enemy cannot find us. There, God can reveal Himself and His great love to us.

I was praying scripture at the church alone one day, reading the Bible as I walked back and forth in front of the sanctuary. Suddenly, I heard the Lord say, "I am going to pour my love out on you." Immediately, a wave from Heaven came down and engulfed me. I began to bend under the weight of it. As this Heavenly power continued, I tried to endure its pressure, but finally had to ask God to stop. I was almost on the floor. His love is so great for us we cannot handle it all in this body.

Worship, reverential awe and adoration, takes place naturally as we come into His presence. Worship takes place in a spiritual realm first then manifests through our daily fellowship of serving Him.

As we surrender ourselves to God in that quiet place, sitting alone and focusing on God and His love, we connect with Heaven, and the enemy cannot enter there. As His Spirit leads us to the Throne of Grace, deeper into the heart of God, everything else disappears, or as the old hymn goes, "The things of this world grow strangely dim in the light of His glory and grace."[4] It is just us and Him. We are welcomed into His presence. He has been waiting for us.

Chapter 22

The Power to Forgive

"Then said Jesus, Father, forgive them; for
they know not what they do..." Luke 23:34

There is none so righteous as Jesus, and no sin so great as to crucify the Son of God, who humbled himself and became a man to show us the way. Yet, He asked forgiveness for the very ones who tortured and crucified Him. He loved them more than He loved His own life. He knew they were blinded and controlled by a force more powerful than they could overcome—a dark spirit realm. Jesus loved the people and defeated the enemy spirit with His precious, sinless blood.

We cannot possibly have this amount of mercy in us except that the Son of God lives in us. By His Holy Spirit, we can be this loving. The Psalmist said to the merciful that they would receive mercy. To forgive is merciful and healing.

I prayed for someone with rheumatoid arthritis, and the Lord told me if that person would forgive the one who offended her, she would be healed. By not forgiving, we subject our physical bodies to illness that doctors cannot heal. Unforgiveness eats a person from within and without.

> "A happy heart is good medicine and a cheerful
> mind works healing, but a broken spirit dries
> up the bones." Proverbs 17:22 (Amplified)

To the one who would not forgive as he was forgiven, the Bible says:

> "And his lord was wroth, and delivered him
> to the tormentors, till he should pay all that
> was due unto him. So likewise shall my heav-
> enly Father do also unto you, if ye from your
> hearts forgive not everyone his brother their
> trespasses." Matthew 18:34, 35

This man did not forgive the debt of another when he had been forgiven a much greater debt. He was delivered to the tormentors for it. When we do not forgive, we deliver ourselves to those who torment us: bitterness, anger, selfishness, etc.

> "But if ye do not forgive, neither will your
> Father which is in heaven forgive your tres-
> passes." Mark 11:26

God is so faithful. His love is never-ending. He wants us to be just like Him. Jesus did what He saw His Father do; so shall we. Forgiveness is healing for body, soul, and spirit.

Wanting to forgive someone can be difficult if we feel that our forgiveness condones the painful act against us. God is not expecting us to condone the wrong, but to let Him handle it.

Recognizing what Jesus did on the cross for us and that there is a force behind evil works that can only be fought by Him, releases us from stepping into the same evil as the offender. Praying for people separates the sin from the person, giving us a new perspective.

God knew this would not be easy. Only those who truly want to be free in their own souls and obedient to Him would even try to forgive others. There have been times when I have had to ask God, "Help me want to, want to forgive." Having the "want to" is sometimes difficult, but it is worth it. The bottom line comes down to this: it is my choice to forgive or not to forgive. When I know the pain I cause myself for not forgiving, I choose forgiveness every time.

The Bible says that God is merciful to those who show mercy.

> "Blessed are the merciful: for they shall obtain mercy." Matthew 5:7

I need a lot of mercy, so there is no other option but to forgive. The merciful are blessed, so forgiving the wrong done to us brings blessing. When we give grace and forgiveness, it will flow back to us in many ways.

Chapter 23
A Holy Zeal

"And, behold, one of the children of Israel came and brought unto his brethren a Midianitish woman in the sight of Moses, and in the sight of all the congregation of the children of Israel, who were weeping before the door of the tabernacle of the congregation. And when Phinehas, the son of Eleazar, the son of Aaron the priest, saw it, he rose up from among the congregation, and took a javelin in his hand; And he went after the man of Israel into the tent, and thrust both of them through, the man of Israel, and the woman through her belly. So the plague was stayed from the children of Israel. And those that died in the plague were twenty and four thousand. And the LORD spake unto Moses, saying, Phinehas, the son of Eleazar, the son of Aaron the priest, hath turned my wrath away from the children of Israel, while he was zealous for my sake among them, that I consumed not the children of Israel in my jealousy. Wherefore say, Behold, I give unto him my covenant of peace: And he shall have it, and his seed after him, even the covenant of an everlasting priesthood; because he was zealous for his God, and made an atonement for the children of Israel." Numbers 25:6–13

Phinehas did what no one else had the courage to do. Even though people were dying all around them, the Israelites would not take action to stop the evil causing it. An idol-worshipping woman had been brought into the sacred camp of God's chosen people. It was a disgrace. God knew her ways would compromise their devotion to Him and idol worship would spread like a cancer among the people. God had higher plans for Israel than to see them walk into the destructive practice of serving powerless false gods:

"Thus, they provoked God to anger with their inventions: and the plague brake in upon them. Then stood up Phinehas, and executed judgment: and so the plague was stayed. And that was counted unto him for righteousness unto all generations for evermore." Psalm 106:29–31

Phinehas stood up against the sin that angered God and caused the plague. He was not one of the oldest—he was only about thirty years old—but he seemed to be one of the wisest . He was the grandson of Aaron, the high priest. There was a spiritual strength in him from God, passed down from his grandfather. What we have in us will increase in our children. There is a spiritual heritage that can be passed on from generation to generation, increasing as it goes when we bring our children up in the ways of God.

Phinehas was not politically correct. He risked his reputation to call out and take action against what was blatantly wrong while everyone else was afraid of offending someone.

There is a line drawn in the sand, and we are making a choice every day which side we will take. Who is on the Lord's side? Let the redeemed of the Lord say so!

If we let sin creep in slowly around us and we do nothing about it, we become desensitized to the wickedness that plagues our society. It is our time to rise up and stop the plague of destruction in our culture, such as addiction, sexual perversion, violence, and more. We can bring back righteousness one step at a time. We are here not to fit in, but to be set apart as God's people:

> "Who gave himself for us, that he might redeem us from all iniquity, and purify unto himself a peculiar people, zealous of good works." Titus 2:14

The things we are to be so zealous about are the good works that God has given us to do. Whether it is in business, school, or ministry, God desires that we burn with passion to do wholeheartedly that which we are called to do as if we were doing it just for Him. Whoever you are working under, let the work you do be as if God Himself were your employer. We are to be the best we can without being lazy or cutting corners. Phinehas was a priest. He was zealous for God and His people. We are called to be kings and priests of God.

All of us know that the greater the goal and the higher the achievement, the greater the discipline. The discipline of a competitive bodybuilder is greater than that of the man who only wants to lose body fat and tone up.

In the military, the discipline of a Special Forces recruit is much greater than of the other enlisted personnel. The disciplines for the higher achievements may seem cruel, mentally and physically, but the result drives the person to greater levels.

It is no different for the one who is diligently seeking God. We study and pray, seeking God, depriving our flesh to increase our spiritual growth, as God leads. We let go of things God says to release and hold to things God says to hold. The world does not understand. We suffer persecution and rejoice that we are counted worthy to do so. Paul encouraged us in his perseverance:

> "I press toward the mark for the prize of the high calling of God in Christ Jesus."
> Philippians 3:14

> ("Press"–*To seek after eagerly, earnestly, endeavor to acquire* [5] *.*)

How can we endure persecution if we have no zeal? We cannot get offended at the very thing God uses to refine us.

We are called to the mountain, to come up higher. We pursue perfection without becoming stressed-out perfectionists.

"Be ye therefore perfect, even as your Father
which is in heaven is perfect." Matthew 5:48

Our perfection in Christ, is trusting God to work through us even with our imperfections. It is a resting place. We do as much as we know God has given us and then, rest in our minds knowing the outcome is up to Him. He does all things well.

God wants us to grow up, to have intimacy with Him. He wants to show us things we have never seen, and to bless us greater than we have ever known. Part of that includes changing us, changing the way we think about God, ourselves, and the way we conduct church. Heaven is excited about God and His plans, we can be too.

When God spoke the verse of 2 Timothy 3:5 to me and made it personal, He was talking about my religion. *You* (me and my denomination) *have had a form of godliness but denied my power.* God is saying, "Are you as sick of religion and your wrong thinking about Me as I am? Are you ready to really know me, no matter what the cost, no matter how uncomfortable it gets, no matter how long you must wait to see the good of it?" Do we know how to wait on the Lord?

Abraham waited twenty-five years for the son of promise to be born. By then, it looked like it was too late. Through all those years, the Bible says Abraham did not give up:

"He staggered not at the promise of God
through unbelief; but was strong in faith,
giving glory to God; And being fully persuaded
that, what he had promised, he was able also
to perform. And therefore, it was imputed to
him for righteousness." Romans 4:20–22

Some of my prayers were not answered for more than twenty years. There are prayers I am still waiting to see answered.

We are to have respect unto the recompense of the reward, as did Moses:

> "Esteeming the reproach of Christ greater riches than the treasures in Egypt: for he had respect unto the recompense of the reward. By faith he forsook Egypt, not fearing the wrath of the king: for he endured, as seeing him who is invisible." Hebrews 11:26–27

Moses knew what was coming was many times greater than where he was. We want instant gratification and no discomfort. It takes more than that; it takes endurance.

I have heard that some law-enforcement recruitment standards have been lowered because there just are not enough people who can meet them.

God does not lower His standards; He raises them. He is coming back for a church without spot or wrinkle, not living in sin and mediocrity, and we are part of it. He raises the bar and we are the ones He is raising.

When Satan lifts his ugly head to deceive more people, God organizes His army of believers and fills them with His Spirit to become more than the enemy can handle,

> "...When the enemy shall come in like a flood, the Spirit of the LORD shall lift up a standard against him." Isaiah 59:19

We, the church, are that standard, the Bride of Christ as an army, zealous for the things of God and His Kingdom.

It is going to take some zealous Christians to bring the Kingdom of God to earth. The fight is not physical against people, it is spiritual, against our own fleshly complacency and laziness. We will be the zealous warriors that take the Kingdom of God by force when we deny our flesh, replace the enemy's lies with God's truth, and seek God's will first:

> "Therefore, I do not run without a definite goal; I do not flail around like one beating the air [just shadow boxing]. But [like a boxer] I strictly discipline my body and make it my slave, so that, after I have preached [the gospel] to others, I myself will not somehow be disqualified [as unfit for service]." 2 Corinthians 9:26–27 (Amplified)

I have seen in a vision the victor coming over the hill, a little bruised, a little battered, but with a big grin, holding the trophy high. It is the invincible Bride of Christ. It is not what we go through that counts; it is that we do not give up. The Kingdom of God is righteousness, peace, and joy in the Holy Ghost. When we deny our fleshly, carnal lusts, we are more joyful, peaceful, and we take on the righteousness of Christ. That is what He did to go to the cross, knowing there was joy on the other side.

Our discipline builds character and brings us into a place where we can be blessed and trusted with the blessing. This keeps us from walking in pride or ungratefulness. When it looks like the journey is too hard, pull up the bootstraps and press forward with joy—a blessing is on the way!

When it seems like the path is going down, rejoice; that is the way up. Letting God have His way humbles the hard, prideful areas of our heart, and He gives grace to the humble. There is great joy on the other side of the battle. There are victories that will amaze us and blessings we thought were only dreams as we continue to stir ourselves up to seek the Lord.

The Lord Himself was very zealous when He saw that man was in desperate need of a savior:

> "And he saw that there was no man, and wondered that there was no intercessor: therefore, his arm brought salvation unto him; and his righteousness, it sustained him. For he put on righteousness as a breastplate, and an helmet of salvation upon his head; and he put on the garments of vengeance for clothing, and was clad with zeal as a cloak."
> Isaiah 59:16–17

He asks no less of us.

Chapter 24

The Invisible and the Visible

"For ever since the creation of the world His invisible attributes, His eternal power and divine nature, have been clearly seen, being understood through His workmanship [all His creation, the wonderful things that He has made], so that they [who fail to believe and trust in Him] are without excuse *and* without defense." Romans 1:20 (Amplified)

M an is without excuse when he does not acknowledge God because His invisible attributes and presence are evident in the things that He created, that which can be seen. God has made Himself known in all of nature. The workings of the universe could not be planned more perfectly, and yet man seeks for a way to explain it as if something had happened by chance. The human anatomy is detailed with intelligence in every minute area of construction, even defending itself from foreign attacks. Childbirth is nothing less than a miracle.

Speaking of Jesus, Paul states:

> "(Jesus) Who is the image of the invisible God, the firstborn of every creature: For by him were all things created, that are in heaven, and that are in earth, visible and invisible, whether they be thrones, or dominions, or principalities, or powers: all things were created by him, and for him." Colossians 1:15–16

To live in the will of God, requires us to understand that the things we cannot see—the invisible—are everlasting. The Bible separates the seen and unseen:

> "While we look not at the things which are seen, but at the things which are not seen: for the things which are seen are temporal; but the things which are not seen are eternal." 2 Corinthians 4:18

What we see with our physical eyes and hear with our physical ears is temporary; we then seek the invisible and eternal things of God. The invisible things of God will last forever: His presence, love, joy, peace, and victory. Our faith, which is the faith in the Son of God, is invisible and it produces the things for which we hope:

"Now faith is the substance of things hoped for, the evidence of things not seen…Through faith we understand that the worlds were framed by the word of God, so that things which are seen were not made of things which do appear." Hebrew 11:1, 3

Even God used faith to make our world.

The world that we see and hear was made by God speaking the word in faith. We are to be just like God and speak the word in faith, producing with our invisible faith visible results.

Much is going on in the spiritual realm. Our words are producing battle outcomes between light and darkness. An unseen guiding light is taking us down the path of life without us always knowing it. Angels stand guard around us with swords drawn and shields uplifted to keep back an unseen enemy while dark forces plot and plan evil schemes. Heaven opens over head to allow our loved ones to get a glimpse of us as they carry our names in prayer to the Throne of Grace. Yes, there is a lot of excitement going on all around us daily that we know nothing about.

Connecting with God brings us into the spiritual realm. We will see eternal truth that is much more real than our temporary knowledge of daily living. Life is exciting because Heaven is excited.

During prayer one morning, I had a vision of Jesus hugging me very tight. He had a big smile on His face. As the hug ended, He took my hand. Together, we began to run toward something huge. I could tell that Jesus was very excited about showing me what was coming. It is still a mystery as to what Jesus was wanting to show me, but I do know wonderful things are going to happen.

Because walking with God is an invisible journey to our physical eyes, it is not seen by those who do not belong to God. Our invisible relationship with God produces great increase in bringing people to the love of God as we get closer to Him. People may not know what draws them to you, but their hunger for a better life will cause them to seek truth. Jesus is the truth, and only He can satisfy a hungry heart. When all the material things lose their excitement, there is One who fulfills the empty heart. To follow the invisible ways of God brings great reward in the spiritual realm. Grace is invisible, but it is felt in the heart and will produce blessings that can be seen, even by others.

Chapter 25
Daniel's Obedience

"In the third year of the reign of Jehoiakim king of Judah came Nebuchadnezzar king of Babylon unto Jerusalem and besieged it."
Daniel 1:1

King Nebuchadnezzar besieged Jerusalem and the Lord gave it to him. The Lord allowed the enemy to take over to bring His people back into obedience to Him. The king asked that certain children of Israel be brought before him, those having wisdom, skill, knowledge of science, and no blemish, to serve him. Of the children were Daniel (Beltshazzar), Hananiah, Mishael, and Azariah, also known as Shadrach, Meshach, and Abednego.

They did not eat of the king's food as they'd been commanded but chose to eat beans and water for ten days. They looked healthier than the others, who had eaten the king's food. As they obeyed the Lord, they became ten times greater than the king's magicians and astrologers. God gave knowledge and skill in all learning and wisdom. Daniel had understanding in all visions and dreams.

God gave dietary laws that made the Jews healthier than all other people. The Hebrews obeyed those laws as part of their worship to their God. Today, we can improve our health by seeking God on how to eat.

King Nebuchadnezzar had a troubling dream that he could not recall. He wanted his magicians and astrologers to tell the dream and interpret it without having any knowledge of what he'd dreamed. Because they could not do it, all the wise men were ordered to be slain. This meant Daniel and his friends. Daniel requested from the king to have some time to seek God for the answer, and it was granted. God revealed the dream and the meaning to Daniel. Daniel praised and blessed God for the revelation.

The king then honored Daniel, also Shadrach, Meshach, and Abednego. He proclaimed Daniel's God was above all others. The king made Daniel a ruler and set Shadrach, Meshach and Abednego in public office.

Obeying God through persecution will cause people to acknowledge our God as their Lord. It will promote us in the spiritual and in the physical.

The king made a gold image that was to be worshipped when music was played. Certain jealous Chaldeans told the king that Shadrach, Meshach, and Abednego were not bowing and worshipping the image, reminding him of his decree that they must be thrown into the fiery furnace. There will always be an enemy to try and destroy the people of God. Our protection is in our obedience, faith, and prayers that He will deliver us.

The king gave Shadrach, Meshach, and Abednego one more chance to worship the image, but they would not. They trusted God. They knew that their God could save them out of the fire, but if He did not, still they would not bow to any other god. The king ordered the furnace to be turned up seven times and commanded the three God-fearing men to be bound and cast into the furnace. The fire was so hot that it killed the king's men who threw in God's boys.

The king was astonished when he looked and saw four men walking around in the fire loosed from their bonds and unharmed. The fourth was like the Son of God.

God will never leave us or forsake us. Right in the middle of the worst trouble, He is there. The fire that the enemy prepared for us has been God's instrument to loose us from bondage. We will come out better than we went in!

King Nebuchadnezzar called Shadrach, Meshach, and Abednego out of the fire. Not a hair of their head was singed, their clothes were not burned, and they did not even have the smell of smoke on them. The king blessed the God of Shadrach, Meshach, and Abednego and decreed that anyone who spoke against them would be destroyed. He then promoted them in the province of Babylon.

We have been through some stuff, but when we trust God, as these guys did, we can come out of it without any repercussions, knowing God went through it with us. We will be wiser, closer to God, with a greater faith.

What a mighty God we serve! Our darkest days produce our greatest victories. They bring the greatest glory to our God, proving His great faithfulness. Though weeping may last for the night, joy comes in the morning. Trusting God brings promotion. It may not come right away, but God sees our obedience in obscurity and rewards us openly.

Chapter 26
The Ministry Within

"Since we have gifts that differ according to the grace given to us, *each of us is to use them accordingly*: if [someone has the gift of] prophecy, [let him speak a new message from God to His people] in proportion to the faith *possessed*; if service, in the act of serving; or he who teaches, in the act of teaching; or he who encourages, in the act of encouragement; he who gives, with generosity; he who leads, with diligence; he who shows mercy [in caring for others], with cheerfulness." Romans 12:6–8 (Amplified)

We want to serve God for whatever He created us. Some people will know from childhood what they are going to do in life. God will put something deep in their spirit to stir up a desire to use the gift He has put in them.

Others, like myself, will have no clue the direction that God is taking with their life.

A woman prophesied over me, when I spoke in Texas, that God could not tell me all that He was going to do with me because I would run. The last thing I ever wanted in life was to be up front, speaking to a group of people.

God created each of us with a specific purpose in mind. The gifts and talents that are given to us are for His glory. We enjoy doing the things that we have worked to perfect and God delights in seeing us operate in our gifts. What becomes uncomfortable is God calling us to function in gifts that we did not know we possessed. God knows what He has hidden deep inside of us and if we only do what is comfortable when God is urging us to be more, we will never experience all for which we were created.

The mother of James and John, with her sons, came to Jesus asking that her sons be allowed to sit on His right hand and His left hand in the Kingdom. These came wanting the up-front position, requesting to be at the top. Jesus said, "You do not know what you are asking." They wanted to be high up on the totem pole, so to speak, but they would never have asked if they knew the suffering they would have to endure with Christ.

> "And he saith unto them, Ye shall drink indeed of my cup, and be baptized with the baptism that I am baptized with: but to sit on my right hand, and on my left, is not mine to give, but it shall be given to them for whom it is prepared of my Father." Matthew 20:23

We will suffer the sufferings of Christ, but instead of letting God use those sufferings to strengthen us in Him, sometimes we turn away from Him and become bitter. We wallow in sorrow for years and, therefore, any ministry that could have been birthed from the experience is delayed.

> "So then, brace up and reinvigorate and set right your slackened and weakened and drooping hands, and strengthen your feeble and palsied and tottering knees and cut through and make firm and plain and smooth, straight paths for your feet [yes, make them] safe and upright and happy paths that go in the right direction – so that the lame and halting limbs may not be put out of joint, but rather be cured." Hebrews 12:12–13 (Amplified)

These are precious keys given to us to know what to do when we feel like we cannot make it anymore. God wants us to be healed for others. This is so we can help someone else get through a tough time. We are healed for the destiny that will further the kingdom of God on earth.

God calls us to look out for each other, to help others not get bitter, hurt, or depressed. When we see someone falling into a pit, the greatest thing we can do is pray for them. We are also to encourage, love, and speak strength into them so they can get back up.

When my son was in college, God was urging me to pray excessively for one of his friends. It seemed to me that none of my prayers for anyone else mattered at this time to God. I finally asked God why I had to keep praying for him so much, but God did not answer. He just kept urging me to pray. After I had been praying for several weeks, the friend was in a terrible car accident in which the trooper told him he should have been killed. My son's friend came out without injury. My son and I both believed my obedience to those urgings from God to pray had saved his friend's life. Our relationship with God and to hear His voice is not just for us but for others also. God put ministry to others in all His children.

Sin does not define a person. Receiving God's forgiveness removes guilt and condemnation, two of Satan's weapons. God's weapons of love and grace are greater and set our feet on the right path.

Fighting against God's love and grace, which is sent to heal us, keeps us from being made whole and produces bitterness and resentment. He is the potter; we are the clay. We were created for Him. He is perfecting us for His use, not ours. We can get up, brush ourselves off, and get going in the right direction.

God spoke to me the night of Andy's death: *"This is the way it is supposed to be. Andy came to live for this time period only..."* God has a plan and it's not ours.

> "The lot is cast into the lap, but the decision
> is wholly of the Lord – even the events that
> seem accidental – are really ordered by Him."
> Proverbs 16:33 (Amplified)

Therefore, we can come under the authorities that are over us in the secular or the spiritual office because God placed them there. Sometimes we are put under less than favorable authority to prove what is in our hearts as it was written of the Israelites when they were sent by

God to wander in the wilderness. Are we obedient to God when people and circumstances are less than favorable where God puts us? We cannot promote ourselves—that is God's business.

Ministry can be birthed out of tragedy and hardships, experiences and encounters. When rough times come, ask God, "What do you want me to learn? How do you want me to handle this?" What you learn and receive from God will be what you use to minister. You will comfort others with the same comfort you received. Without our own difficult times, we have nothing with which to comfort others. We release to God feelings of hurt and anger, so the ministry can be birthed or begin to operate.

We embrace God's word:

> "And we know that all things work together
> for good to them that love God, to them who
> are the called according to his purpose."
> Romans 8:28

When we are asking for a ministry, a mantle, or an up-front position, we do not know what we are asking. We cannot seek to be seen in a position, or to be promoted—seek God. He will take us to the perfect place in Him.

> "But seek ye first the kingdom of God, and his
> righteousness; and all these things shall be
> added unto you," Mathew 6:33

God gives us grace to wait on Him.

Chapter 27

Intimacy

"...let the one who boasts boast in this, that
he understands and knows Me [and acknowl-
edges Me and honors Me as God and recog-
nizes without any doubt], that I am the LORD
WHO PRACTICES LOVING KINDNESS, JUSTICE
AND RIGHTEOUSNESS ON THE EARTH, FOR IN
THESE THINGS I DELIGHT," SAYS THE LORD."
Jeremiah 9:24 (Amplified)

God wants us to know Him personally, to have a relationship with Him, to grow in knowledge of who He is
and how He thinks, His will and His ways. This is achieved
as it is with any other person we want to know: we spend
time with Him, read what He has written in His word, and
listen to Him.

It is the most extraordinarily wonderful, ongoing quest
there is: to know Him. It is like finding Him yet still knowing
there is so much more to find.

"O the depth of the riches both of the wisdom and knowledge of God! how unsearchable are His judgments, and His ways past finding out!" Romans 11:33

Even more than this, there is the immeasurable love that flows in this union that pulls the heart to something beyond what words can describe, then takes that soul to a place that does not exist in the realm of human knowledge. We begin to long for God's presence.

"...I will seek Him whom my soul loveth..." Song of Solomon 3:2

"Draw me, we will run after thee..." Song of Solomon 1:4

The woman in the Song of Solomon proclaims, "He has drawn me, and I must run after Him." How can we find Him? He can be found in the early quiet hours of the morning, when to others it is still night, but to the bride and the bridegroom there is sweet fellowship.

"...Early will I seek thee: my soul thirsteth for Thee, my flesh longeth for Thee..." Psalm 63:1

He is found in the quiet prayer, praise, and silence as the soul enters in to His presence. He whispers His love and delight to the longing heart, expressing His own joy. There is a satisfying of the soul's depth that would not be known except that He calls and the soul answers. Still, He is not found, He is eternal.

"...Christ, in whom are hid all the treasures of
wisdom and knowledge," Colossians 2:2–3

In meditation on the Lord and His word, comes an insatiable hunger for more of Him.

The book of Hosea reveals how God came to redeem His beautiful bride, Israel, His beautiful creation. She was soiled, bruised, and dying, but He lifted her head and called her His own when no one else wanted her. The state she was in was of her own doing. She had played the harlot, running after other lovers. No true love was ever provided by them; in fact, the opposite came—disappointment, hurt, loss, pain, and death of a dream. Separation and rejection came from all she sought. This was the outcome of the bride who left her first love. We are also that bride.

Love appeared on the scene that had no conditions, no requirements except to be received. There was supernatural power in Love. Love knew no bounds and exceeded human knowledge. Sweeping up the bride, Love destroyed the destroyer and set the apple of His eye free from the clutches of sin and death. God is Love.

All that is required of the bride, us, His people, is to receive this outpouring of adoration from our Creator and let Him become our one true Love. Believe that He came just for us and accept His life and His righteousness as our own. The bride is magnificent in His sight. He covers us in grace, crowns us with loving kindness, and seats us on the throne beside Him. Our eternity with Him has begun.

If you have never accepted Jesus Christ as your Savior and would like to do so now, you can pray something like this:

> Lord Jesus, I know that I am a sinner. I ask You to come into my heart. I receive Your sacrifice and forgiveness for all my sins. I make You my Lord and Savior. Thank You for saving me!

If you prayed this prayer from your heart, you are now a saved child of God! Spend time in prayer with God every day, read your Bible, and find a church that teaches God's Word. May God guide you and keep you in His loving care.

Notes

1 Chapter 12: Humility, the Way Up

"Humility, the Beauty of Holiness," by Andrew Murray, 1884, this printing 2000 (Christian Literature Crusade, USA, P.O. Box 1449, Fort Washington, PA 19034, Pocket Companion Edition, edited and reset 1991, page 7, 51, 54, 55

2 Chapter 18: A Virtuous Woman

Blue Letter Bible, Strong's Concordance, H2428, https://www.blueletterbible.org/lang/lexicon/lexicon.cfm?Strongs=H2428&t=KJV&ss=1

3 Chapter 20: Our Own Worst Enemy

Blue Letter Bible, Strong's Concordance, G4561, "Outline of Bible Usage," IV, https://www.blueletterbible.org/lang/lexicon/lexicon.cfm?Strongs=G4561&t=KJV

4 Chapter 21: Spirit, Soul, and Body

"Turn Your Eyes Upon Jesus," by Helen H. Lemel, 1922.

5 Chapter 23: A Holy Zeal

Blue Letter Bible, Strong's Concordance, G1377, https://www.blueletterbible.org/lang/lexicon/lexicon.cfm?Strongs=G1377&t=KJV